**Busy Kids, Hap|**

a four-in-one set by Deb Graham

| Many of Deb Graham's Books Now Available in audiobook form! |

**Busy Kids, Happy Kids**

Deb Graham

© Copyright and All Rights Reserved 2018 by the author, who doesn't share well.

**Four books by Deb Graham in one set**—everything you need to inspire a young one in cooking, science, and crafts is in your hand. If you're a parent, teacher, homeschooler, scout leader, or love a child in any capacity, read on!

## Awesome Science Experiments For Kids

Easy, wow-factor science projects a child can do with minimal help with materials found at home, and some fun snack ideas for hungry explorer.

## Quick and Clever Kids' Crafts

Loaded with gift-giving-worth craft ideas for all ages, plus a bonus section on swaps, those little pieces of artwork on a safety pin. If you're a scout leader, parent or teacher, you're in luck!

## Kid Food On A Stick

Not just for kids---any food tastes better on a stick Every meal of the day, fancy desserts and healthy snacks are easy to serve on a stick, and will tempt even picky eaters.

## Hungry Kids Campfire Cookbook

Not your average beans and weenies. Wholesome recipes to wow any child (or adult!) Cooking methods include hot dogs in milk cartons, omelets in baggies, sandwiches on a stick, jello in a river, eggs in peppers, muffins in orange peels, eggs in paper bags, and of course some innovative foil packets. Delicious for any camping trip or your own kitchen!

# Awesome Science Experiments For Kids
## by
## Deb Graham

© Copyright 2013

## A bored child is a sad thing

Children are endlessly curious about the world around them.  A child who can look at their surroundings and wonder "what would happen if..." will be brighter than most, and certainly more interesting to be around.  Encourage questions, and let the children make guesses as to the outcomes.

Here in your hand are ideas to teach and entertain at the same time. I've used these games, activities, and science projects in large and small groups. It's great to see young eyes light up, as they grasp a new concept  They will naturally want to expand the projects, trying new ways to do it differently next time.  Some experiments will 'fail', but there is no failure if a child learns something

Because young scientists get hungry, I've added a **BONUS section** of kid-friendly, easy snack recipes  Some are sure to become favorites.

## Group Games .................................................................. 10
### Non Elimination Musical Chairs ...................................... 10
### Lemon Derby ........................................................... 11
### Penguin Feet Relay .................................................... 11
### WHAT IF...? ............................................................. 12
### Line Tag ................................................................. 15
### Blanket Volleyball ..................................................... 15
## Outdoor Science Experiments: ........................................... 17
### Odors in Nature ........................................................ 17
### Sundial .................................................................. 17
### Film Canister Rockets ................................................ 18
## Non-Messy Science Experiments ........................................ 19
### Personal Numbers ..................................................... 19
### Learn About Inertia ................................................... 19
### Are You A Box? ....................................................... 19
### Catching Sound Waves ............................................... 20
### Rainbows in the Dark ................................................ 20
## Science Experiments with Water ........................................ 22
### Pet Cloud ............................................................... 22
### Ice Cube On A String ................................................ 22
### Hot Meets Cold ....................................................... 23
### Waves in a Bottle .................................................... 23
### Skin Senses ........................................................... 24
### How Many Pennies? ................................................. 24
### Carbonated Liquids .................................................. 24
### Carbonated Fruit ..................................................... 25

| | |
|---|---|
| Static Electricity and Magnets | 26 |
|    Crystal Mountains | 26 |
|    Magnets | 26 |
| Paper Science | 27 |
|    Structural Integrity | 27 |
|    Color Wicking | 27 |
|    Invisible Ink | 28 |
| Messy Science Projects | 29 |
|    Liquid or Solid? | 29 |
|    Acid or Alkali? | 29 |
|    Mister Grassy Head | 30 |
|    Gravity Bean Sprouts | 31 |
|    Blow Up A Balloon | 31 |
|    Play with Polymers   (GOOP) | 32 |
|    Make a Crystal Snowflake! | 33 |
| BONUS    SNACKS for Hungry Scientists | 35 |
|    Banana Chiller | 35 |
|    Jammy Pockets | 35 |
|    Pretzel Melts | 36 |
|    Mini Bagel Pizzas | 36 |
|    Smiles | 36 |
|    Tics on a Latrine Seat | 37 |
|    Moose Lips | 37 |
|    Pudding Cones | 37 |
|    Fruit Skewers and  Dip | 38 |
|    Apple Moons | 38 |

Nutty Pretzel Wands ....................................................... 38

Octopus Hot Dogs .......................................................... 39

Tiny Cookie Pizzas ......................................................... 39

Wormy Apples ................................................................ 39

Cold Fried Eggs .............................................................. 40

Salad- on-a Stick ............................................................ 40

Cinnamon Snowflakes ................................................... 41

Cheese Quesadilla ......................................................... 41

Indoor S'mores ............................................................... 42

S'macos ......................................................................... 42

## _Group Games_

### Non Elimination Musical Chairs

*I can't stand it when a child is crying in a corner, feeling rejected because they are "out." This is a fun group game for any age, and no one is "out!" How many people can be stacked on just a few chairs? My personal record is the entire Church Junior Sunday School on three folding chairs.*

Place chairs, back to back, in a line, one less that there are people playing, as for typical Musical Chairs. Start the music, and have everyone walk around chairs. When the music abruptly stops, each person must find a place to sit. If there is no seat available, they must find a lap. Remove one chair, then start the music again, as players walk around. Remove a chair each time the music stops. As chairs ---not people—are removed, sitting becomes more of a challenge Keep playing and removing chairs until the whole group is piled on just 2-3 chairs. Admire how creatively the group figured out the best placement. Is it better to pile smaller people on bigger laps? Or to hold up others?

## WHAT IF...?

*What If...is a fun game for rainy days, although it works just as well outdoors as indoors. It saved me one evening at camp, when the rain just did not let up. A group of grumbling complainers forgot they were miserable and wanted to go home, replaced by laughter in no time flat. The giggles went on long after the game ended*

*It's easier than it sounds, and often hilarious for any age group I've played What If with grade-schoolers, teens, and adults, and it works every time. You may want to play multiple rounds by setting aside the used papers, and writing new questions and answers on fresh papers. Only requirement...the players must be able to read and write.*

For this group game, have everyone sit in a circle, with a pen or pencil, a small stack of scrap paper cut into squares about 2-3 inches, and something firm to write on (hardcover children's books are great). Each person silently writes "what if" on the paper, then continues the question, making certain it fits the What If format. When done, fold each paper in half, and place in a basket or bowl. When each person's paper is in the container, pass it around the circle, with each person drawing a paper out. Don't be concerned about whose paper is drawn. Read the question, silently, then turn it over and respond on the back.

When all are done, read the paper in this order: first person reads the question (not the answer) aloud. The second person reads his/her *answer* (not the question) aloud. Then person #2 reads his/her question, and the next person in the circle reads the answer on their paper, and so on. Continue around the circle, ending with the last person reading her *question*, and the first person reading her *answer*. The round ends when the last person read their <u>question,</u> and the first person reads their <u>answer.</u>

### *Example:*

**Person #1**'s question reads "<u>What if</u> everything is purple when we wake up tomorrow?"

Person #2's question (which is not read at first ) was "<u>what if</u> our canoe leaks?" Her (totally appropriate) answer is "then we'll have to walk all the way back to camp, dripping wet."

When read aloud, the order is like this: person #1 reads his/her question. "<u>What if</u> everything is purple when we wake up tomorrow?" and the second person reads #1's answer: ""then we'll have to walk all the way to camp, dripping wet." The second person then reads $2's question : "<u>what if</u> our canoe leaks?" to which the third person may read, " put that messy puppy in the back yard!" ( the answer to #4's question about a furry pet).

*Just try it---you'll catch on fast and it'll likely end up being a favorite game at any gathering or party!*

## Lemon Derby

Have teams roll a lemon with a stick to the finish line, in a relay race fashion. Lemons wobble more than any ball. It's harder than it sounds!!

## Penguin Feet Relay

Make a pair of paper plate 'shoes' for each team. For each shoe, use 1 and ½ paper plates. Place half plate upside down on whole pate, making a large pocket. Line up edges, staple together. To play, have each team form a line, side by side. On cue, each team member slips on the paper plate shoes, runs to a designated spot, then back, tagging the next in line. Pass the shoes to the next team member. If shoes slip off, runner must stop and put them back on. First team to complete the course wins.

## Blanket Volleyball

*This game is just like normal volleyball, but using a blanket to toss the ball over the net   It requires teamwork.*

Divide players into two teams, and give each a similar-sized blanket.  Each team stands around their team's blanket, holding the sides to pull it taut. The 'serving' team should start by placing the ball on the blanket, letting their blanket loosen  then pulling it  tight so it 'throws' the ball over the net.  The other team then uses their blanket to catch the ball, then throw it back. Scoring is the same as ordinary volleyball.

## Line Tag

*Play on outdoor tennis court or basketball court. 10+ players*

Pick two volunteers to be "it" for the game.

Everyone else needs to be spaced out on the court lines. The player's goal is to not be tagged by those who are "it". Everyone, including those who are "it", can only stay on the court lines- if someone runs off the line or jumps to another line, then they have to sit down and become a "block" (you'll have to watch for this).

The people who are "it" try to tag other players, shouting "Block!" as they are touched. Once a person is tagged, he/she must sit down at that exact spot and become a block. The player running on the lines cannot run past the players who are blocks - only the people who are "it" can run past the blocks and tag everyone else. Last person standing wins the game.

## *Outdoor Science Experiments:*

### **Odors in Nature**

Send children outdoors in teams of two or three, with set boundaries and a five minute time limit. Each team writes down odors they noticed, then reports back. Odors might include rotting wood, wet grass, a nearby trash, rain, flowers or plants. Talk about what caused the odors. Would it be different if the weather changed?

### **Sundial**

Tape a *paper* to a flat surface in full sun. Secure *a pencil* upright in the center, using a small bit of *play dough*. Mark a line where the pencil's shadow falls. Check back later. Has the line moved?

### **Film Canister Rockets**

*Outdoor activity Be careful to step away after you cap it, as it could hurt your face as it flies up*

Acquire several *35mm film canisters* from a photo developing shop (they're free, and discarded; just ask).

Add varying amounts of *water* to each canister. Drop 1/4 *Alka Seltzer* tablet into each canister, cap tightly, and set lid side down on hard service. Step back.

*Which goes off first? Does adding more or less water make them fly higher? If you glue on paper fins, does the flight path change?*

## *Non-Messy Science Experiments*

*well, less messy, anyway!*

### Personal Numbers

How old are you? How many toes do you have? What is your weight? Height, arm diameter? How far is it from you finger to your thumb? How long is your foot? What other numbers can you measure? Numbers are all around us

### Learn About Inertia

Spin a *raw egg* and a *hard cooked egg* on a table. Which one spins longer? Which wobbles more? Why do they behave so differently?

## Are You A Box?

Lie down on the floor. Spread your arms out to the sides, holding still. Have a friend set *four books,* touching each of your feet and fingertips. Carefully sit up, and turn to put your feet where your hands were, and vice versa. Is it the same distance? Try this with people of different ages; pre-schoolers, adults, teens. Does it change?

## Catching Sound Waves

Tie two lengths of 14" *cotton string/twine* to the flat side of a *metal coat hanger.* Wrap end of string around your index fingers. Stick index fingers in your ears. Bump the hanger into something; a table, wall, coat, etc. Bump something else. Did it sound the same, or different?

## Rainbows in the Dark

Get several *glass crystals*, perhaps borrowed from a chandelier. Turn off the lights, and shine a small *flashlight* at the crystal while holding it. Can you see a full color spectrum? What happens if you move the light beam around?

## _Science Experiments with Water_

### Pet Cloud

Pour a tiny bit of *hot water* into an *empty soda bottle*. Shake. Drop a lit *match* into the bottle, cap quickly. Squeeze the bottle gently, over and over. Look through the bottle. See your pet cloud moving?

### Ice Cube On A String

Submerge *an ice cube* in a glass of *water* for a second or two. Let it float to the top. Place a *string* on top of the ice cube, with enough extra to drape over edge of glass. Sprinkle a little *salt* over it. Count to ten. Pick up the loose end of the string. The ice will lift right out of the glass!

**How it works:** The salt is the secret ingredient. It lowers the freezing temperature of water, so it easily melts ice. That' s why people in cold climates spread it on the road after a snowfall — and why the ocean rarely freezes. When you sprinkle the salt on the ice, some of the ice melts back into water, which is absorbed by the string. Seconds later, the water in the string refreezes (the ice underneath the string never touches the salt, so it doesn't melt). The result? The string is frozen to the cube, allowing you to pick it up.

## Hot Meets Cold

Fill a large clear jar three-fourths with lukewarm *water*. Fill a baby food jar with very cold water and few drops *blue food color*. Fill a second baby food jar with hot water and *red food color*. Cover both with foil and secure with tight rubber bands. Poke pencil-lead-sized hole in foil. Set both jars into larger jar. Watch what happens as the cold and hot water leak out. Where do they go?  Why?

## Skin Senses

Pour warm *water* into a bowl, hot into another, icy cold into a third. Dip one hand into the hot water, and another into the cold water. Then dip both hands into the warm water at the same time. What did it feel like?

## How Many Pennies?
Set a small *juice glass* on a table. Fill into almost to overflowing with *water*. Drip more in with a spoon, but don't let it spill over. Now, guess how many p*ennies* you can add without it spilling? If you slide them carefully under the water's surface, you may be surprised at how many can fit.

## Waves in a Bottle

Fill a baby food jar halfway with *cooking oil.* Fill with *water.* Do the layers mix? Add a few drops of *food color.* Cap tightly. Swirl until the color bursts as it hits the water. Can you tell why it acts like it does?

## Carbonated Liquids

*Any beverage can be carbonated, even chocolate milk Look at a hardware store's plumbing department for an adaptor, or you can buy ready-made ones online. Take a 2 liter bottle to the store with you, to get the right size. Vinyl tubing also comes from hardware stores, or pet store's aquarium section. Set up the tubing-adaptor part to be sure it fits snugly before mixing ingredients.*

The idea here is to carbonate any beverage by connecting two 2-liter (or 1-liter) bottles together with a length of clear vinyl tubing. Put the drink to be carbonated in one bottle, and equal parts baking soda and vinegar in the other. Quickly attach tubing with adaptor to catch the carbon dioxide. As the baking soda and vinegar react, CO2 is produced, which moves through the tubing into the other bottle. Let set until fizzing slows. Shake the vinegar-baking soda bottle once, to be sure it's done fizzing. Shake up the bottle with the beverage to dissolve the CO2. There You've got carbonated orange juice, eggnog, or whatever else you choose.

## Carbonated Fruit

*Takes overnight, but the wow-factor reaction is worth it!*

Place soft *fruit* (grapes, berries, apples, melon chunks) on a plate inside a cooler. Add a few ounces of *dry ice,* and *tape* cooler securely, sealing all openings. Let set overnight or up tp 24 hours. Untape and eat fruit.

## Static Electricity and Magnets

### Crystal Mountains

Rub *an inflated latex balloon* with a *wool cloth.* Hold balloon over a plate with plain (dry) gelatin on it. Be careful not to let the balloon tough the gelatin. Listen. Can you heard tiny pinging sounds as the gelatin flies up to meet the balloon? Drag the balloon almost touching the gelatin to make crystal mountains. Rub with wool cloth if it stops picking up gelatin.

## Magnets

Shred some dry *steel wool* into a *shoe box lid*. Drag a *magnet* on the underside of the box lid. What happens? Try drawing a simple shape ---maybe a face—in the lid first. Can you control the steel wool enough to decorate it?

## **Paper Science**

## Color Wicking

Fold a paper coffee filter into quarters. Draw a heavy dot at the point with a washable black or purple marker. Dip the tip into water. Watch the colors as they spread upward. Besides being as fun introduction to chromatography, these make pretty art materials when dry!

## Structural Integrity

Fold identical copier-type *paper* into a round cylinder, a wide pleat, a fan shape, a tri fold zig zag, and a pup tent shape. Tape each to hold its shape. Stand each on end. Carefully set a thin children's *book* on each. Add more books, very carefully, until the shapes collapse. Which was stronger? Which held more books?

## Invisible Ink

Write or draw with lemon juice or milk on water paper, using a small paintbrush. Use broad strokes, with minimal details. Let dry, then carefully iron or hold over bare (hot) light bulb to reveal the message.

## Messy Science Projects

*Messy is not a bad word Plan ahead, and cover your work surface, or go outdoors*

### Liquid or Solid?

Combine several cups of *corn starch* and enough *water* to make very thick paste in a flat pan (9X13 works well). What does it do when you try to play with it? It flows like liquid, breaks like a solid. Which is it?

### Acid or Alkali?

Shred *red cabbage* and cook in 2 cups water, covered, until cabbage is soft. Reserve cabbage for another purpose, such as lunch. Put a tablespoon of cabbage water in each paper cup. Add small amounts of different household materials to each, and record color changes. Try *grapefruit juice, lemon juice, baking soda, Epsom salt, alcohol, cooking oil, liquid soap, milk, tomato juice,* etc. If they turn pink, they are acids. If they turn green, they are alkali, or base.

## Mister Grassy Head

*How do seeds grow?*

*You'll need a nylon knee high stocking, grass seeds, potting soil, a baby food jar, and googly eye, plus fabric scraps or markers*

Put a few seeds, maybe a teaspoon, in the toe of the stocking. Add in a few spoons of potting soil, making sure the combination of seeds and soil is a little larger than the mouth of the baby food jar. Pour about an inch of water into the jar.

Tie a knot in the stocking below the soil to keep the seeds and soil in, or rubber band it shut. Completely soak the soil/seed ball. Place the stocking leg part in the jar, with the soil filled 'head' above the jar. The soil part is the head and the grass will look like hair as it grows. The excess stocking will be placed in the baby food jar to soak up water. The baby food jar is the body. Add eyes and decorate the jar to make Mister Grassy Head's body. Place in a warm windowsill and watch it sprout in just a few days!

## Blow Up A Balloon

Put a few spoons of *baking soda* into a *latex balloon*. Put an inch of *vinegar* into small empty *soda bottle*. Fit the balloon over the bottle, letting baking soda fall in to vinegar. Why did it do that?

## Gravity Bean Sprouts

*Does gravity affect what direction a bean grows? Use any whole dry bean from your pantry, or buy a seed packet.*

Take an empty jar, and line it with a couple of layer of paper towels. Dampen with water. Carefully slide several dry beans between paper towel and jar walls. Set it somewhere dark and warm for a couple of days, checking to be sure it does not dry out. The top of the refrigerator, under a towel, is a good spot.

Note which way the root sprouts; you may even wish to mark it with a marker on the glass. When the sprout is a couple of inches long, put it out in the light. Set the jar upside down, and leave it to grow longer. Did the sprout change direction? What happens if you lay the jar on its side? Has the sprout's color changed? Why?

## Play with Polymers    (GOOP)

*Find Borax where laundry detergents are sold*

4 oz. white school glue

2 cups water

1 teaspoon powdered Borax

Pour the glue and water into a bowl. Mix. Add 1 teaspoon Borax to rest of water and mix well. Stir both mixtures together. You should have a thick mass in a liquid. When the glob has formed into one chunk, pour off the remaining liquid. The mixture thickens when you knead, stretch, and play with it. *CAUTION: Do not eat.* Avoid carpet, fabric, and furniture.

## Make a Crystal Snowflake!

*See how crystals are formed in this fun activity Experiment with food coloring, and hang your finished crystal snowflake as a great looking decoration. Boiling water is required, so adult help is advised.*

You need: About 12 inches of string, a wide mouth jar, white pipe cleaners, boiling water, Borax, pencil, blue food color (optional)

Cut a white pipe cleaner into three sections of the same size. Twist these sections together in the center so that it forms something like a six-sided star. Make sure the points of your shape are even by trimming them to the same length.

Tie one point of the pipe cleaner to the string, and the other end to a pencil.

Mix 3 tablespoons Borax for each cup of boiling water, making enough solution to fill the jar an inch from the top. Stir to dissolve the Borax, but don't worry if some of the borax settles at the base of the jar. If you want your snowflake to have a bluish cast, add in a few drops of blue food color now.

Set the pencil on the rim of the jar, and submerge the snowflake into the liquid, being careful not to burn yourself.

Put the jar somewhere undisturbed. Check it a few times through the day. Can you see crystals forming yet? By the next day, your snowflake will be covered in sparkly crystals.

Remove from solution, and set to dry on paper towels. Remove the pencil, and hang by the string.

## *BONUS   SNACKS for Hungry Scientists*

*Science is fun, but can make you hungry Here are some easy, fun snack recipes to share as you think of your next experiment.*

### Banana Chiller

Combine one banana, 1 cup milk, 2 teaspoons sugar, and 5-6 ice cubes in a blender. Blend until smooth. Serve immediately.

### Jammy Pockets

Roll out refrigerated pizza dough to 1/4 inch thick; cut into 3-inch rounds. Dollop with cream cheese and jam. Brush the edges with beaten egg, fold in half and press to seal. Brush with egg and sprinkle with sugar. Poke a hole in each; bake 20 minutes at 400 degrees F. Let cool a bit before eating.

### Pretzel Melts

Sandwich small slices of cheddar between mini pretzels. Put on a parchment-lined baking sheet and bake about 10 minutes at 425 degrees F. Serve with mustard.

## Mini Bagel Pizzas

Arrange mini bagels on cookie sheet, cut side up. Spread a spoonful of bottled spaghetti sauce on each bagel. Sprinkle shredded mozzarella cheese on each, and top with 2-3 pepperoni slices. Bake at 450 degrees until cheese is melted and bubbly. Next time, vary ingredients...peppers, onion, cooked chicken or sausage, etc.

## Smiles

Core apple. Slice into wedges, spread with hazelnut spread (like nutella), then add a row of small marshmallows (teeth) closest to the peel. Top with another apple wedge & Smile!

## Tics on a Latrine Seat

Spread **cream cheese** on a cored **apple** ring, add **raisins** in a ring

## Moose Lips

Cut red apple into eight wedges, top to bottom, and trim away seeds. Spread one side of each with peanut butter or caramel dip. Sandwich 4-5 chocolate chips or mini marshmallows between 2 apple wedges for teeth.

### Pudding Cones

Mix instant pudding according to package directions in a zipper bag. Spoon into ice cream cones, sprinkle with chocolate chips. Eat immediately.

### Fruit Skewers and Dip

*Suggestions: banana, apples, kiwi, grapes, melons, berries, pears, mango, stone fruits*

Cut various fruits into cubes, about the size of a grape. Thread on bamboo skewers.

Mix 1 cup sour cream and 2 tablespoons each brown sugar and lemon or lime juice. Serve skewers with the dip.

### Wormy Apples

Spread apple wedges with peanut butter. Wrap gummi worms around each.

### Apple Moons

Slice an apple into crescents. Spread with peanut or almond butter and press granola on top.

## Nutty Pretzel Wands

Spread peanut butter on the top few inches of a long pretzel rod. Roll in chopped peanuts.

## Tiny Cookie Pizzas

vanilla wafer or sugar cookie

cream cheese thinned with a little honey and vanilla extract

fruits cut into tiny interesting shapes; thin slices, ovals, bits

Spread cream cheese mixture on wafers, then artistically top with fruit.

## Cold Fried Eggs

*. If you arrange carefully, these look like fried eggs on toast*

Set a slice of pound cake on a plate. plop a spoon of whipped cream in the center, then arrange a canned peach half, cut side down, on top of the cream.

## Salad- on-a Stick

String any assorted raw vegetable in bamboo skewers. Serve with puddle of bottled salad dressing for dipping.

Cucumber, cherry tomatoes, zucchini, carrot rounds, broccoli, cauliflower, snow pea pods, celery chinks, pineapple cubes, bell peppers, all work great

## Cinnamon Snowflakes

*Remember the paper snowflakes you made in first grade? Same concept here.*

Carefully fold a flour tortilla in half, then half again. Using a scissor, cut out small shapes from the sides, taking care to leave part of each fold intact. Unfold. Place on cookie sheet. Brush with butter (or spray with cooking spray). Sprinkle with cinnamon-sugar mixture. Bake at 350 until barely golden.

## Indoor S'mores

Spread marshmallow creme on a graham cracker, sprinkle with chocolate chips, top with another cracker.

## S'macos

*Are these really better than S'mores??*

Sprinkle one flour tortilla with about 2 T chocolate chips and 8-10 mini marshmallows. (don't overdo –these are very messy!) . Heat on griddle or grill until chips are glossy. Fold to eat.

## Cheese Quesadilla

*1 flour tortilla*

*3 T grated cheddar cheese*

*2 T chopped ripe olives*

*bottled salsa*

Sprinkle cheese and olives on tortilla. Broil or heat in flat pan over medium heat until cheese is melted. Fold in half. Dip in salsa

**A Plea:**

I hope you find some projects of interest in my book. More importantly, I hope it inspires you to take time with the kids in your life, to teach and enjoy them  Be sure to read the other books in this series.

**Please take time to leave a five-star review of this book. It'll take you under four minutes, and can be anonymous if you'd prefer.  I greatly appreciate it**

Thanks!

## ***Kid Food On A Stick***

by Deb Graham

©copyright 2014    All Rights Reserved

# Kid Food On A Stick

by Deb Graham

*What Kind Of Stick?* ............................................................... 60
*Food-On-A-Stick tips:* ............................................................ 63
Breakfast On A Stick ................................................................ 65
    **Cinnamon Rolls On A Stick!** ........................................... 65
    **Donut Holes With Berries On A Stick!** ........................ 66
    **Donut Holes On A Stick!** ................................................. 68
    **Sausage Pucks on A Stick ( with Magic Sauce )** ...... 68
    **Magic Sauce** ........................................................................ 69
    **Crunchy French Toast And Any Berry On A Stick** ... 69
    **Sausage and Biscuit On A Stick With White Sausage Sauce** ..................................................................................... 70
    **Biscuit Logs With Sausage Gravy!** ............................. 72
    **Sausage Gravy** ................................................................. 72
    **Scotch Eggs On A Stick!** ............................................... 73
    **Silver Dollar Pancakes On A Stick** ............................ 74
*Lunch On A Stick* ................................................................... 75
    **Corn Dogs On A Stick** ................................................... 75
    **Baked Mozzarella Bites On A Stick with Homemade Marinara Sauce** ................................................................. 76
    **Pizza Pinwheels On A Stick** ........................................ 77
    **Pizza On A Stick** ............................................................. 78
    **Mini Calzones On A Stick** ............................................. 79
    **Fancy Peanut Butter Pinwheels On A Stick** ............ 79
    **Terrific Tiny Meatballs on A Stick!** ............................. 80
    **Meat Pies On A Stick** ..................................................... 81

Empanadas On A Stick ! ..................................................82
Amazing Pie Crust ..........................................................84
Lunch Munch Kabobs! ....................................................84
Curly Sausages On A Stick ...........................................85

*Dinner On A Stick*..............................................................86
Grilled-Not- Fried Chicken On A Stick! .....................86
Chicken Chip Sticks ......................................................87
Barbecued Chicken-Pineapple On A Stick! ...............88
Burger Logs On A Stick ..............................................89
Fishy Fishy On A Stick ...............................................90
Fish Cake Balls On A Stick ! ......................................91
Bul-Ko-Kee (Korean BBQ).........................................92
Pioneer Drumsticks! .....................................................93
Grilled Shrimp On A Stick! .......................................94
Porcupine Meatballs On A Stick ! .............................94

*Side Dishes On A Stick*......................................................95
Grilled Summer Vegetables On A Stick! ....................96
Baked Sweet Potatoes On A Stick ! ..........................96
Italian Caprese Salad On A Stick ! .........................97
Grilled Fruit On A Stick ! ............................................98
Grilled Pineapple On A Stick! ....................................98
Grilled Peaches On A Stick!........................................99
Walking Salads On A Stick .........................................99
Bacon Tot Bites On A Stick ....................................100

*Snacks and Appetizers On A Stick*..............................101
Mozzarella Pastry On A Stick! ..................................101

Sausage Pretzel Pops On A Stick with Pesto! ........ 102

Cold Shrimp and Grapes On A Stick ....................... 103

Wrapped Smoked Bites On A Stick .......................... 103

Crunchy Ravioli On A Stick ! ..................................... 104

Ham and Melon On A Stick ....................................... 104

Cucumber Rolls On A Stick! ...................................... 105

Peaches and Pesto Mozzarella On A Stick! ............. 106

Mini Cheese Balls On Pretzel Sticks ........................ 107

*Desserts and Sweets On A Stick* ............................... 108

Fruit On A Stick ( and dip ) ........................................ 108

Hand Pies On A Stick ! ............................................... 108

Amazing Pie Crust dough (*see Empanadas On A Stick recipe*) ................................................................ 109

Cinnamon Snails On A Stick ..................................... 110

Apple Wedges on A Stick .......................................... 110

Stuffed Strawberries On A Stick ............................... 111

Chocolate Chip Cake Mix Cookies On A Stick ! ..... 112

S'mores Cookies On A Stick ..................................... 113

Jammy Cookies On A Stick ....................................... 114

Hot Cocoa On A Stick ................................................ 115

Itty Bitty Nutty Grapes On A Stick! ........................... 116

Ice Cream Potatoes On A Stick! ............................... 117

Frozen Bananas On A Stick ...................................... 117

Come on, admit it. There's a certain magic about food-on-a-stick. It makes any meal taste like instant summer Stuck in gloomy wintry weather? Put dinner on a stick, spread out a blanket on your floor and ---instant picnic From breakfast to midnight snacks, kids love food on a stick.

Kids love cotton candy, corn dogs, frozen fruit bars, and lollipops....but let's get back to wholesome, nutritious eat-for-dinner food. I've included some treats, but most of these recipes are downright good for you...just don't mention that to the kids

The recipes in this book are ideal for a tea party, picnic in the yard, sleepover, lunchboxes, and of course, family dinners at home. Most of these recipes are easy enough for an older child to make on their own, but even a toddler can poke a stick into a grape. Stringing food on a stick looks like play, but it's serious business to a budding chef

### *What Kind Of Stick?*

The variety of stick you choose depends on the type of food, the age of the eaters, and whether it's cooked or cold. For example, you may want to use a fancy frilled pick for a party, a craft stick for littler hands, and reserve lollipop sticks for cold items. Teens can handle any type of stick, but toddlers are safer with blunt-ended sticks. Heavier foods do better with sturdier sticks. Some foods are best served with *two* sticks, side by side, to prevent the food from spinning as it's eaten Some sticks are edible, without added ingredients: cheese sticks, pretzel sticks, breadsticks, carrot and celery sticks make easy sides, and fit the theme effortlessly

Look for various sticks in cooking supply stores, craft stores, or any place that sells cake decorating materials.

Each type of stick has advantages, and disadvantages. Let's look at them, one by one.

**Metal shish kebab skewers** are reusable, washable, sturdy, and they don't burn or break. They do get hot, though. Available in straight, curved, and circular shapes. These are best for sturdy grilled foods, such as meats and vegetables.

**Bamboo skewers** are readily available, flexible, compostable, come in multi packs, and are cheap. For younger children, simply snip off the point before serving. These are fine for grilled or cold foods, so long as they are not too heavy. May use two, side by side, if twirling food is an issue. Be sure to soak the skewers before cooking, to prevent flare ups.

**Bamboo chopsticks** are disposable, renewable, sturdy, don't roll, are not sharp, and come in convenient pairs. Ideal for heavier foods.

**Toothpicks and frilled picks** are good for small one-bite items, and just fine for dipping. They make any food more appealing. Be careful with younger children, as they are sharp.

**Plastic cocktail swords** are festive and fun, but useable only for cold or precooked foods, such as fruits and dips. They are best used for one-bite items.

**Pretzel sticks** are small, and ideal for appetizers. They have no waste, since the food is eaten stick and all Pretzel sticks do just fine in the oven. If you're cooking with meat, prop the pretzel end on a ball of foil to avoid soaking up any grease from meat as it bakes

Thin **wooden cocktail forks** have two or three tines, which makes it easier for slippery foods to stay put, such as shrimp. They're good for single-bite foods, especially nice for dipping, and best stuck on prepared foods just before serving.

Curved **bamboo knots and hors d'oeuvres sticks** come in different shapes and colors, and make any food fancy enough for a party  Add stick after food is prepared

**Wooden craft sticks**, flat or notched, are the go-to stick for small hands. Inexpensive packs of 50 or 100 are available in craft stores.  Avoid colored ones. Food cannot spin or slide around on craft sticks. They are fine for sturdy food, and hold up to baking, or grilling (be sure to soak them first!)

**Paper lollipop sticks**, found with cake-decorating supplies, are pretty for cold desserts. For cookies or hand pies, add sticks after baking; they burn.  Add a little ribbon bow for bake sales.

**Cinnamon sticks** are especially nice for French toast and fruit. Buy whole cinnamon sticks from a craft store or bulk section of a grocer; the sticks sold in the spice area are more expensive.

For meats, and meatballs, a **rosemary sprig** makes a pretty party presentation. Cut a slit in the meat to make insertion easier.

### *Food-On-A-Stick tips:*

~~Don't feel obligated to completely fill a stick---foods look appealing, even perched on the end, and it's a lot easier to eat with a handle.

~~Wooden and bamboo sticks used for grilled or baked recipes should be soaked in water for 30 minutes, to lessen the chance of the sticks burning while the food cooks.

~~Hosting a party? Sticks are also a great way to display and serve food for a crowd. Guests feel valued, simply because you bothered to present their food on a stick, instead of plopped on a plate.

~~Many recipes here are very flexible; they are more method than precision. Not all have precise measurements...if you want a single serving, there you go; want more, add more ingredients. Keep it fun, and be creative!

~~Picky eaters are more likely to sample a new food if it's on a stick. Great chefs know "we eat with our eyes first."

~~Of course, enlisting the kids in the cooking process is great---it's part of the fun, and they feel like they're needed (which they are!), as well as making their appetites surge. Even timid eaters can't resist food they helped prepare

~~Feel free to mix categories---if you make it smaller, it's an appetizer, larger is a meal, a fancier stick makes it party-worthy, and of course the "rules" about what's acceptable for breakfast flew out the window years ago. You can mix and match meals, too; you may decide grilled peaches are a dessert one day, or side dish the next week. Entirely up to you!

Breakfast On A Stick

*Start the day off with some fun! Whether it's your own kids, or a sleepover full of hungry young ones, this is the way to go. Start with these recipes, then use your creativity to make up others*

## Donut Holes With Berries On A Stick!

*This is a classy breakfast, perfect for a sleep over, and couldn't be easier Of course you may substitute other fresh fruits, cut to donut-hole size as needed. Have more time? Make your own donut holes Recipe follows*

fresh strawberries, raspberries, blackberries, and/or other berries, washed, caps removed

donut holes

vanilla yogurt

Simply alternate berries with store bought donut holes on a skewer, and serve with vanilla yogurt for dipping.

## Cinnamon Rolls On A Stick!

*Better than a bakery, and not much more effort. These are just right for a sleepover. You can even make them the night before; cover and chill until time to bake.*

2 1/4 cups flour

1 envelope yeast

1 1/2 teaspoons sugar

2/3 cup very warm milk

3/4 teaspoon salt

3 tablespoons butter, softened

*Filling*: 1 /4 cup brown sugar

1/3 cup raisins

1 /4 cup butter, softened

Combine 1 cup flour, yeast, sugar and salt in a large bowl. Add very warm milk and 3 tablespoons butter. Mix until well blended, about 1 minute. Gradually add enough remaining flour to make a soft ball. It will be slightly sticky. Knead on a floured board, adding additional flour if necessary, until smooth and elastic, about three minutes. Let rest five minutes.

Preheat oven to 375 degrees. Roll the dough out to a 1/4-inch thick rectangle. Spread remaining butter on rectangle, leaving 1 inch border on one long edge. Sprinkle brown sugar and raisins over butter. Roll up like a rug, towards unbuttered edge. Pinch edge to seal. Cut slices, 3/ 4 inch thick. Place slices on greased baking sheet. Let rise 20 minutes. Bake until golden, about 15-20 minutes. Insert chopsticks or craft sticks.

TIP: Cut 18" dental floss or thread. Wiggle floss under end of roll, and cross ends, pulling tight to cut slices. Makes a smooth cut, and won't flatten as knife could.

### Donut Holes On A Stick!

*If you're making these for the Donut Holes with Berries recipe, add the stick <u>after</u> frying. They're quite delicious on their own, too*

refrigerated biscuits (the cheap ones work best; avoid the expensive butter-flecked grands type)

oil for frying

cinnamon/sugar mixture

Cut each biscuit into four pieces. Arrange each dough piece on a wooden cocktail fork or craft stick. Fry at 350 degrees until golden, turning once. Drain on paper, then sprinkle with cinnamon sugar. Eat warm.

## Sausage Pucks on A Stick  ( with Magic Sauce )

*The dough will seem crumbly, but work it in your hands and it will come together. Add a teaspoon or two of water at a time if you get desperate. The Magic Sauce is also delicious on lunchmeat or veggie sandwiches and hot dogs.*

1  pound raw bulk sausage (Italian, sweet, breakfast style, or hot)

4 cups grated sharp cheddar cheese

3 cups baking mix (such as Bisquick)

Combine sausage, sharp cheese, and biscuit mix in a bowl. Work with your hands until it comes together. Shape into balls about ping-pong ball size, and flatten to 1 inch thickness. Cook in dry frying pan over medium heat until golden, turning a few times.  Impale each on a stick for easy dipping.

## Magic Sauce

*This tastes very complex, but couldn't be easier. I learned it working at a country club in college, where the chef jealously guarded the recipe; fancy, super-easy secret recipe, just for you! It's also great on cold sandwiches.*

Stir together:

1 cup mayonnaise     1 1/ 2 tablespoons yellow mustard

## Crunchy French Toast And Any Berry On A Stick

4 slices thick bread

3 eggs

3 tablespoons sugar

3/4 cup milk or half-and-half

3 cups crushed corn flakes

dash cinnamon

3 tablespoons butter

fresh berries

Preheat oven to 375 degrees. Melt butter in a skillet. Whisk eggs, sugar, milk, and cinnamon together. Dip each slice of bread into egg mixture, allowing time for each to absorb the mixture. Coat each slice evenly in the cornflakes, pressing to adhere. Melt butter in a skillet. Pan fry the slices in the butter, turning once, until golden. Transfer to baking sheet. Bake 4-6 minutes to crisp. Cool just enough to handle. Cut each slice into bite-size cubes, and string on a skewer, alternating with fresh berries. Serve with syrup for dipping, if desired.

## Sausage and Biscuit On A Stick With White Sausage Sauce

*A hot breakfast with a warm gravy for dipping –yum Add a drink and some fruit, and it's a complete breakfast*

1 pound breakfast link sausage

1 tube refrigerator biscuits

dash black pepper

1 cup milk

Cook sausage until almost done in a skillet. Slide a craft stick into each link. Wrap each link in a biscuit, and place seam-side down on a baking sheet. Bake at 325 degrees until browned. While they bake, make the **White Sausage Sauce**:

**White Sausage Sauce:** drain all but 4 tablespoons sausage drippings ; add butter to make 4 tablespoons if sausage is too lean.

Stir in 4 tablespoons white flour and a dash of black pepper, scraping up the browned bits. Stir in milk and stir until bubbly. Serve sausage and biscuits on a stick with Sauce.

## Biscuit Logs With Sausage Gravy!

*Who can resist homemade biscuits with gooey sausage gravy? You can also use a biscuit mix or refrigerator tube-type biscuits, but this recipe is almost as fast and far better. You can use a food processor if you choose not to grate the butter. Don't add all the soured milk at once; you may not need it all.*

2 cups flour

2 teaspoons baking powder

1/2 teaspoons baking soda

1/2 teaspoons salt

4 tablespoons cold butter, grated

2/3 cup milk stirred with 1 tablespoon lemon juice or vinegar

Stir together dry ingredients with grated butter until coarse. Stir in most of the sour milk, adding just enough to bring the dough together. Knead ten times, and form into 10-12 logs of roughly even size with floured hands. Insert a craft stick into each log, from the end. Bake at 400 degrees until just golden. Serve with Sausage Gravy for dipping.

## Sausage Gravy

*If gravy is thicker than you'd like, add a splash more milk as it cooks.*


1 pound bulk sausage; mild, hot, or Italian

1/3 cup all-purpose flour

4 cups milk (low fat, whole, or mixture of milk and half-and-half)

1/2 teaspoon salt

2 teaspoons freshly ground black pepper

3 tablespoons chopped fresh parsley


Break apart sausage, as it cooks, into small bits. Cook until no longer pink. Stir in flour a spoon at a time, until mixed well. Add milk, stirring constantly. Sprinkle in salt, pepper and parsley. Cook 3-5 minutes, stirring constantly, until bubbly and thick. Serve hot in small bowls with the Biscuit Logs, for dipping.

## Scotch Eggs On A Stick!

*Sturdy chopsticks or craft sticks work well for these fun baked breakfast eggs. They also make great bedtime snacks for a sleepover!*

4 hard cooked eggs, peeled (cook a few minutes less if you prefer softer yolks)

1 pound bulk pork sausage

flour to coat

3/4 cup dry bread crumbs

1 egg, beaten

Flatten sausage into four equal patties.

Roll each peeled egg in flour to coat, then wrap sausage around egg, pinching to completely cover. Insert wooden chopstick or craft stick into egg. Dip each into beaten egg. Coat with bread crumbs. Bake at 400 degrees on ungreased cookie sheet for 35 minutes, until crust is nicely browned.

## Silver Dollar Pancakes On A Stick

*Be sure to stack the pancakes; sticks won't stay on if you try to impale them sideways*

Pancake batter ( the add-water mix is fine for this recipe)

fresh strawberries, raspberries, or blueberries

Whipped cream and syrup for dipping


Prepare batter as directed on the package. Cook 2" wide pancakes, flipping once. Stack 2 pancakes, and alternately put stacks with a berry or two onto a craft stick or bamboo skewer. Repeat. Serve with warmed syrup and whipped cream.

## _Lunch On A Stick_

*The lines between lunch and dinner food are pretty blurry. Let's say lunches are smaller, and maybe less effort to make, shall we? Certainly feel free to mix it up.*


### Fancy Peanut Butter Pinwheels On A Stick

*Sure, p b & j is fine, but for entertaining, such as a tea party, this is much fancier Substitute almond butter if desired.*

4 sandwich bread slices

4 tablespoons smooth peanut butter

4 tablespoons fruit jam or jelly

Remove bread crusts. Flatten bread slices with a rolling pin. Spread peanut butter and jelly on each slice, and roll up like a log. Cut each roll into four pieces with a serrated knife. Insert frilled pick or appetizer stick to hold spirals tight.

## Corn Dogs On A Stick

*Tastes just like the ones at the carnival Choose a sturdy stick; a craft stick or bamboo chopstick is best. Want minis? Just cut each hot dog in thirds before placing on the stick*

1 cup yellow cornmeal

1 cup flour

1/2 teaspoon seasoned salt

4 tablespoons sugar

1 tablespoon baking powder

1 egg, beaten

1 cup milk

1 lb all beef hot dogs, patted dry

oil for frying

Pat each hot dog piece dry, and place on stick. Preheat oil to 350 degrees. Combine cornmeal, flour, salt, sugar and baking powder. Stir in egg and milk. Transfer batter to a deep container, such as a drinking glass. Dip each hot dog to coat, and fry, stick and all, until golden. Drain on paper towels.

## Baked Mozzarella Bites On A Stick with Homemade Marinara Sauce

*If you're not going to cook the mozzarella today, freeze it, then place in zip-type bags for up to three months. Parchment makes clean up a snap!*

1 pound string cheese, cut into fourths

milk

panko or Italian bread crumbs

2 cans whole or diced tomatoes, drained, juice reserved

2 tablespoons olive oil

4 cloves garlic

chopped fresh herbs (your choice: oregano, parsley, basil, etc) to taste

salt and pepper

Place cheese sections on a skewer, or coffee stirrer. Dip in milk, then roll in crumbs. Freeze on baking sheet at least 30 minutes. Bake mozzarella bites at 400 degrees on parchment lined baking sheet 6-10 minutes until golden and gooey. Serve with warm marinara sauce

**Marinara Sauce:** combine remaining ingredients, simmer 15-30 minutes, adding reserved juice if it seems too thick. Serve sauce for dipping

## Pizza Pinwheels On A Stick

*Pizza spirals—oh, yum Fancy enough for a party. An even easier version follows*

1 3/4 to 2-1/4 cups flour         3/4 teaspoon salt

1 envelope yeast                  2/3 cup very warm water

1 1/2 teaspoons sugar             3 tablespoons oil

1/2 cup pizza sauce or crushed tomatoes with oregano and garlic

1 1/2 cups grated mozzarella cheese

your favorite pizza toppings: pepperoni, cooked sausage, peppers, mushrooms, olives, etc...

Preheat oven to 425°F. Prepare baking sheets with parchment paper

Combine 1 cup flour, yeast, sugar and salt in a large bowl. Add very warm water and oil; mix until well blended, about 1 minute. Gradually add enough remaining flour to make a soft ball. It will be slightly sticky. Knead on a floured board, adding additional flour if necessary, until smooth and elastic, about three minutes.

Roll the dough out to a 1/4-inch thick rectangle. Layer on the sauce, cheese, and toppings, leaving some cheese exposed to hold the pizza pinwheels together. Roll into a log, starting at the long end. Cut into 1/ 2 thick slices. Set on parchment covered baking sheet, leaving space for the dough to puff as it bakes. Insert craft sticks or wooden chopsticks. Rest for ten minutes. Bake for 12- 15 minutes, or until golden brown with melted cheese.

## Pizza On A Stick

*These cute flat pizzas are even easier than the Pizza Pinwheels Mix up the toppings to suit your tastes, or let the kids make their favorite combinations.*

Preheat oven to 425 degrees. Prepare dough as directed in Pizza Pinwheels recipe. Roll pieces of dough into 3 inch rough circles, 1/ 2 inch thick. Add craft stick. Place on greased baking sheet. Spread sauce, cheese and toppings, leaving slim crust at edges uncovered. Rest ten minutes. Bake until bubbly and bottom of crust is just golden.

## Mini Calzones On A Stick

*Little pizza pouches It's fun to have each child choose their favorite toppings*

Make Pizza On A Stick, except fold each circle in half and crimp edges before baking. Add stick after baking.

## Terrific Tiny Meatballs on A Stick!

*These are delicious, with either ground beef, ground chicken, or turkey Pass the sauce for dipping. Sturdy craft sticks work great here.*

1 pound ground beef, chicken, or turkey

1 slice bread, torn

1/4 cup chopped fresh parsley

2 eggs, lightly beaten

1 tablespoon whole milk

1 tablespoon ketchup

3/4 cup grated Romano or Parmesan cheese

3/4 teaspoon each salt and black pepper

jarred marinara sauce *(or use recipe in Baked Mozzarella Bites)*

Preheat oven to 375 degrees. Combine all ingredients. Form balls, about walnut size. Place two meatballs on each craft stick. Bake on baking sheet until no longer pink inside, about 7-9 minutes. Serve with marinara sauce for dipping.

## Meat Pies On A Stick

*Made with frozen bread dough, these tasty pies are fun to make and eat They're tasty warm or cold, and just right in a packed lunch. Use sturdy sticks; craft sticks are best.*

1 lb ounces ground beef

1 small yellow onion, finely chopped

1 small potato, diced

8 ounces frozen mixed vegetables, thawed

1/4 cup fresh parsley leaves, chopped

1 dill pickle, chopped

1 loaf frozen bread dough, thawed

1 egg, beaten

Brown the beef with the onion and potato. Drain grease. Season with salt and pepper. Stir in vegetables, parsley and pickle. Set aside. Cut the dough into 8 pieces. Roll each into a circle, about 1 3/ inch thick, on a lightly floured board. Transfer to greased baking sheet. Place a craft stick on each, with end sticking out 2-3 inches. Evenly divide the meat mixture on the center of each circle. Dab water on the edge of the dough, and fold in half, crimping with fork to seal. Brush with beaten egg. Bake at 375 until golden.

## Empanadas On A Stick !

*Portable Mexican meat pies are ideal for a lunchbox or after-something snack They freeze and reheat well, so make plenty. Don't forget to soak the craft sticks first*

1 pound lean ground beef

1 onion, diced

2 cloves of garlic, minced

salt and pepper

1 teaspoon ground cumin

1/4 teaspoon ground cinnamon

1/8 teaspoon ground cloves

1 / 4 cup salsa

1 cup canned tomatoes

1/4 cup raisins

1 egg, beaten

**Amazing pie crust (recipe follows)**

Brown the beef with onion and garlic, breaking apart as it cooks. Drain fat. Stir in salt, pepper, cumin, cinnamon, and cloves. Add the salsa, tomatoes and raisins, and simmer until raisins are softened. Cool at least 10 minutes.

Preheat oven to 425 degrees. Prepare **Amazing Pie Crust.** Roll half of the dough between 2 sheets of waxed paper. Cut into 2 inch rounds, and place on baking sheet. Plop a tablespoon of filling on each circle, and add a craft stick. Roll out rest of dough, and cut circles. Brush edges of filled circles with beaten egg. Set top circle on each, and crimp tightly with a fork to seal. Cut tiny slit for steam to escape in each empanada. Brush remaining egg over empanadas. Bake 12-14 minutes, until golden brown. Serve warm or at room temperature. Variation: bake without stick, then insert paper lollipop stick after baking

## Amazing Pie Crust

*Yes, this recipe is not technically on-a-stick, but it's a versatile crust for just about any filled pie you want to put on a stick This super easy, fabulous, flakey, foolproof, brag-worthy pie crust will win raves, sweet or savory, on a stick, or not. Makes two 10 inch pie crusts, or enough for about 24 2 –inch pies on a stick*

2 2/3 cups flour

1 1/2 teaspoons salt

3 /4 cup oil

4 1 /2 tablespoons cold water


Stir together flour and salt. Measure oil and water in the same cup, and pour over flour, all at once. Stir just until dough comes together, leaving some streaks. Roll out between 2 sheets of waxed paper. Fill as desired, and bake at 425 degrees until golden. (hint: use leftover scraps for **Cinnamon Snails On A Stick**)

## Lunch Munch Kabobs!

*A nice change of pace from plain old hot dogs. Be sure to soak bamboo skewers in water at least 30 minutes.*

hot dogs or Polish sausages

pineapple (fresh or canned)

hot dog buns

Cut hot dogs or Polish sausages into 1" chunks. String on skewers with pineapple chunks. Grill until hot through. Serve in hot dog buns

<u>Variation</u>: substitute ham cubes for hot dogs. Add mushrooms or zucchini chunks instead of pineapple.

## Curly Sausages On A Stick

*These are easy enough for a child to help make, and fun to eat Dip in barbecue sauce or ketchup.*

Polish sausages

refrigerated crescent roll dough

Cut Polish sausages in half, and stick each on a craft stick. Unroll dough, and pat creases together. Cut strips one inch wide. Wrap each sausage, leaving spaces between dough. Place end-side down on baking sheet. Bake at 375 degrees until browned. Serve with ketchup and mustard.

## *Dinner On A Stick*

### Not- Fried Chicken On A Stick!

*Every kid likes breaded chicken, and this is healthier than fried  The grill adds smoky flavor, but on a rainy day, of course you can use the oven. Be sure to soak the skewers so they won't burn.*

4 boneless, skinless chicken breast halves, pounded 1/2 to 3/4 inch thick

salt and pepper

garlic powder

2 tablespoons cooking oil

4 tablespoons barbecue sauce

1 1/2 cups plain dried bread crumbs

Cut chicken into strips, 1 inch wide.  Weave them onto bamboo skewers. Sprinkle lightly with salt and pepper and garlic powder. Preheat grill.  Stir together the barbecue sauce and oil, and brush each chicken skewer with mixture. Roll in bread crumbs, patting to coat. Grill the chicken skewers until they're no longer pink inside, about 2 to 4 minutes per side, turning a  couple of times. Serve with more barbecue sauce.

## Chicken Chip Sticks

*You can vary the flavor of these Chicken Chip Sticks by using different flavored potato chips. Try barbecue flavor chips, cheddar & sour cream, chili-lime, dill pickle, spicy pepper, salt & vinegar potato, sour cream and onion, even ketchup flavor They're great with plain salted chips, as well. Kids will love smashing the chips. Put them in a zip-type bag, pressing as much air out as possible, and tell them to stomp them to crumbs.*

4 chicken breast halves, cut into 1/2 inch cubes or strips

1 egg, beaten

2 tablespoons milk

2 cups crushed potato chips, any flavor

Preheat oven to 350 degrees. Beat egg with milk in pie pan. Arrange chicken on soaked skewers or craft sticks. Dip in egg-milk mixture, then roll in crushed potato chips, coating well. Bake on greased baking sheet 10-15 minutes, turning once, until lightly brown and no longer pink inside.

## Barbecued Chicken-Pineapple On A Stick!

1 cup ketchup

1/4 cup soy sauce (low sodium is best)

1/4 cup honey

1 /4 cup brown sugar, packed

1 tablespoon prepared mustard

2 garlic cloves, smashed to flatten

3 Tablespoons lemon juice

1- 2 1/2 pound chicken, cut into 1 1/2 inch chunks (or use breasts or thighs)

fresh or canned pineapple, cut into 1 1 /2 inch chunks

2 tablespoons olive oil

Stir together first six ingredients, and cook over medium heat until thickened, about ten minutes. Remove large garlic pieces. While sauce cooks, alternate chicken cubes and pineapple on soaked bamboo skewers or wooden coffee stirrers. Brush with olive oil.

Divide sauce into two bowls; reserve one for dipping. Grill skewers, basting with the barbecue sauce, until cooked through, about 10 to 15 minutes.

## Burger Logs On A Stick

*They're not pretty, but are they good!- They're easier to grill if you shape them ahead and freeze, at least an hour or so.*

1 lb Ground beef

1 packet onion soup mix

4 strips bacon

Season 1 lb ground beef with a packet of dry onion soup mix. Form into 4 hot-dog shaped logs. Wrap each log with a slice of bacon, at an angle to cover most of meat. Secure with toothpick, if needed. Insert a wooden craft stick for a handle. Grill over medium heat, turning a few times, until cooked through. Serve with ketchup and mustard.

## Fishy Fishy On A Stick

1 pound mild whitefish, such as cod or haddock, cut into cubes

1 tablespoon creole seasoning

1 /4 cup flour

2 eggs, beaten

2 cups crushed cornflakes

cooking spray


Preheat oven to 350 degrees. Coat baking sheet with cooking spray. Arrange fish cubes on wooden coffee stirrers or bamboo skewers. Combine flour and creole seasoning in a shallow dish. Beat egg in another dish, and place crushed cornflakes in a third shallow dish. Dip fish in flour and creole seasoning, then in egg, and in cornflakes to coat. Place on baking sheet. Coat with cooking spray. Bake until the fish is opaque in the center and the breading is golden brown and crisp, about 10 minutes, turning once.

## Fish Cake Balls On A Stick !

*Use cod, salmon, mackerel, or any leftover cooked fish. If you're using cooked fish, add it to the potatoes after they are drained. Just be sure to remove the bones*

2 large potatoes, peeled and cubed

1 pound cod or other fillets, cubed

1 tablespoon butter

2 tablespoons minced onion

¼ cup minced celery

1 tablespoon chopped fresh parsley

1 egg

oil for frying

3 tablespoons pickle relish

4 tablespoons mayonnaise

Simmer potatoes in water until almost tender. Add fish cubes and cook until fish is done. Drain well.

Stir in onion, parsley, celery, relish, and egg ; mash the mixture together until the texture is like play dough. Shape the mixture into golf ball sized balls, and insert craft sticks.

Heat oil in a large skillet to 350 degrees. Fry the fish balls, turning twice, until golden brown. Drain on paper towels before serving. Mix relish and mayonnaise together for dipping.

## Bul-Ko-Kee   (Korean  BBQ)

*Bul-Ko-Kee is Korea's national dish. It resembles teriyaki, and it'll quickly become a favorite Serve on cooked rice. The beef is easiest to cut when it is semi-frozen*

1 lb tender beef steak, cut into cubes or thin slices

1 /2 cup soy sauce

3 T sugar

2 T vegetable oil

1 tsp black pepper

3 green onions, finely chopped

2 cloves minced garlic

Cut semi-frozen meat into cubes or thin slices. Combine rest of ingredients, and marinate for 45-minutes (or up to a day).  Thread beef on coffee stirrers or bamboo skewers. Grill or pan sear just until cooked through. Serve with hot rice.

## Pioneer Drumsticks!

2 pounds any combination of ground beef, ground pork, bulk sausage, or ground chicken

1 cup corn flakes, crushed

2 eggs

salt, pepper, and garlic powder to taste

medium onion, minced

Mix ingredients thoroughly and divide into 12 equal portions. Wrap around the end of the sticks, making the roll long and thin, leaving a couple of inches of stick exposed for a handle. Cook over coals, turning frequently, until cooked through. Eat off the stick, like a drumstick.

## Grilled Shrimp On A Stick!

*Grilled shrimp---it must be summer!*

1 pound uncooked medium shrimp, peeled and deveined

1/2 cup seasoned breadcrumbs

2 tablespoons olive oil

2 garlic cloves, crushed

1/2 lemon, zested and juiced

salt and pepper to taste

Pat shrimp dry. Toss with olive oil, garlic, and lemon juice and zest. Add breadcrumbs and toss to coat. Thread the shrimp onto skewers. Grill over medium heat, turning once, until shrimp is opaque in the center and the crumb coating begins to brown.

## Porcupine Meatballs On A Stick !

*The rice sticks out like little porcupine quills!*

1 pound ground beef

1 egg

1/2 cup raw rice

1 4/ onion, finely chopped

1 clove garlic, mashed with 1/2 teaspoon salt

1/2 teaspoon ginger (fresh grated or dry)

water or broth

Sauce:

one can cream of chicken soup

1/2 cup milk

Combine meat through ginger. Form firmly packed balls, about walnut ball size. Arrange in deep skillet, and add enough water or broth to reach a third of the way up the meat balls. Simmer, covered, adding more liquid as needed, 15 minutes, until no longer pink in center. Heat soup with milk. To serve, place a stick in each meatball, and eat with the dipping sauce.

## *Side Dishes On A Stick*

*Round out any meal Some may pass for appetizers, snacks, or even dessert. Use the recipes as jumping-off point to inspire new combinations. Be creative*

### Grilled Summer Vegetables On A Stick!

*Your anti-veggie kids may forget they "hate that", when it's presented on a stick Older kids can help arrange the vegetables on the sticks.*

assorted summer vegetables: summer squash, cherry tomatoes, sweet peppers, zucchini onions, etc, cut into bite sized pieces

bottled Italian dressing

Soak bamboo skewers in water 30 minutes. Arrange a variety of vegetables on skewers. Grill until tender, turning and basting frequently with dressing.

## Baked Sweet Potatoes On A Stick !

*A nutritious vegetable that tastes like dessert? Pass the plate, please!*

Sweet potatoes or yams, peeled

maple syrup

Cut sweet potatoes or yams into 2 inch chunks. Place each on a coffee stirrer or cocktail fork. Arrange on parchment-lined baking sheet. Brush with maple syrup. Bake at 350 degrees until tender, basting with maple syrup twice more.

## Italian Caprese Salad  On A Stick !

*Is this a fancy party food, or a salad? Couldn't be easier, or prettier — fresh mozzarella balls, cherry tomatoes, and basil leaves. No chopping, dicing, or slicing required.*

mozzarella balls or cubes

cherry tomatoes

fresh basil leaves

Olive oil

lemon juice

Thread on a skewer or cocktail fork, in this order: one fresh mozzarella ball, one cherry tomato, one basil leaf, folded. That's it Serve with olive oil and lemon juice drizzled over.

## Grilled Fruit On A Stick !

*Mix this up with other fruits; plums, papaya, mango, and apples work well.. Pass the napkins*

Cut fresh pineapple and peaches into bite-sized cubes. Alternate on a bamboo skewer. Grill until tender with slight char marks. Sprinkle with cinnamon sugar mixture.

## Grilled Pineapple On A Stick!

*Is this a side dish, or dessert? Either way, it'll be a favorite! It's even more delicious with vanilla ice cream*

Whole pineapple, peeled and cored

brown sugar

optional: cinnamon, chili powder, ground ginger

Cut away the outer parts of a whole pineapple, and slice horizontally into one inch thick slices. Grill until golden, turning once. Rub top side with a brown sugar, or a mixture of sugar and spices. Cook another minute, turn, rub other side with sugar and grill a few seconds more.

Variation: cut long spears instead of slices.

### Grilled Peaches On A Stick!

*Nectarines are just as good Remember to soak the skewers in water first, so they don't catch fire.*

Cut peaches into bite-sized squares. String on bamboo skewers. Grill, turning frequently, until a few charred spots appear. Drizzle with honey.

### Bacon Tot Bites On A Stick

*Easy, tasty side dish or appetizer*

frozen hash brown bites ("tater tots")

bacon

cheddar cheese (optional)

Preheat oven to 425 degrees. Wrap each potato bite with a slice of bacon, cutting off overlap. Place on baking sheet, seam side down. Bake until bacon is crisp. Stab each with a toothpick, or frilled pick. Serve with ketchup. **Variation**: slide a small cheddar cheese cube under each bacon slice before baking.

## Walking Salads On A Stick

*Kids "won't eat their vegetables"? They haven't tried these Add cooked chicken cubes and cheese for a full lunch. Choose any of the suggested vegetables*

Cucumber chunks

cherry tomatoes

zucchini or other summer squash in 1" slices

carrot rounds

broccoli heads, cut into bite-sized pieces

cauliflower, cut into bite-sized pieces

fresh snow pea pods

celery chunks

pineapple cubes

mini sweet peppers or bell peppers, cut into bite-sized pieces

2" wedges of lettuce or cabbage

good quality bottle salad dressing

String assorted raw vegetables on bamboo skewers. Serve with puddle of bottled salad dressing for dipping.

## **Snacks and Appetizers On A Stick**

*Call it party food, and kids are more likely to try new things These are also fun for after school, after sports, after anything They're also great for parties, and even adult events.*

### **Mozzarella Pastry On A Stick!**

*Crisp, elegant, cheesy---what more do you need?* Marinara sauce is great for dipping

frozen puff pastry dough, thawed

string cheese mozzarella sticks, cut in half

sliced pepperoni

marinara sauce

Preheat oven to 425 degrees. Unroll dough. Cut into rectangles, 3 inches across the narrow side of dough. Lay 3 slices pepperoni and cheese in the center f rectangle. Roll up, tucking in sides as you go. Bake, seam side down, until puffed and golden. Insert lollipop stick or chopstick.

## Sausage Pretzel Pops On A Stick with Pesto!

*These are fun for a picnic, or a party Dip in pesto, then chow down, stick and all Freeze leftover pesto; it's delicious as a dipping sauce or over pasta*

1 1/2 cups washed spinach leaves

3/4 cup fresh basil leaves, packed

1/2 cup almonds

1/2 cup grated Parmesan cheese

4 cloves garlic, peeled and quartered

 tablespoons olive oil

juice AND zest from half a lemon

1 1 2/ lbs chicken or pork sausage, cut in 2" pieces (try other flavors: chicken-apple is good!)

pretzel sticks

Combine all but sausage and pretzels in food processor. Blend until nearly smooth. Set aside. Cook sausage in a pan until cooked through. Impale each sausage piece with a pretzel stick, and drizzle with pesto.

## Cold Shrimp and Grapes On A Stick

*The title pretty much tells the story of these fun party foods They're great with a pineapple cube instead of the grapes, to mix it up.*

Thread cooked, peeled shrimp on fancy cocktail skewers, with a single green grape in the curve. Chill. Oh, Yum

## Wrapped Smoked Bites On A Stick

*Makes a lot of bites for a crowd in a hurry Even faster if the kids are enlisted to help assemble these tasty snacks. Like pigs-in-a-blanket, only better, and you get to eat the stick!*

cocktail-sized smoked sausages

mustard

refrigerator biscuits

thin pretzel sticks

Separate refrigerator biscuits. Tear each in half, between layers of dough (you'll end up with two rounds). Place a sausage on a biscuit, and add a thin streak of mustard down the side. Wrap the dough around the sausage, pinching to seal, leaving ends exposed. Bake on ungreased baking sheet at 350 until dough is golden. Add pretzel stick to each.

## Crunchy Ravioli On A Stick !

*Fancy appetizer or fast lunch. Serve with jarred sauce, or the **Marinara Sauce** recipe in the **Baked Mozzarella Bites** recipe*

Frozen ravioli, any variety

egg, beaten

Italian seasoned bread crumbs

non-stick cooking spray

Marinara sauce


Thaw frozen ravioli. Dip in beaten egg, then in Italian bread crumbs, to coat. Insert stick. Place on baking sheet, and spray liberally with cooking spray. Bake at 375 degrees until crisp. Serve warm with sauce

## Ham and Melon On A Stick

*Easy, terribly elegant, and the kids will love the salty-sweet combination. Fancy enough for a tea party!*

Honeydew (or other melon), balled

cooked ham slices, folded into quarters

Using a melon baller, cut balls from the melon. Put the folded ham on a skewer or cocktail fork. Top each with a melon ball, and arrange upright in a fancy glass.

## Cucumber Rolls On A Stick!

*Elegant enough for a party, simple enough for a picnic lunch in the park. Next time, try adding bacon bits*

cucumber, unpeeled, sliced into thin long ribbons with a mandolin or vegetable peeler

4 ounces feta cheese

1 block cream cheese, softened

2 tablespoons fresh parsley or other herbs

Stir together cheeses and herbs. Place a small amount on the end of a cucumber slice, and roll up. Secure with toothpick, frilled pick, or bamboo cocktail fork. Roll the rest. Chill for at least an hour to firm up the filling.

## Nutty Pretzel Wands

Spread peanut butter on the top few inches of a long pretzel rod. Roll in chopped peanuts.

## Peaches and Pesto Mozzarella On A Stick!

*Try the pesto recipe in Sausage Pretzel Pops with Pesto recipe, or used jarred pesto in a pinch. Substitute small fresh mozzarella balls if you'd prefer*

peaches, cut into rough cubes

mozzarella cheese, cut in similar sized cubes

pesto

Alternate peaches and cheese on skewers, Place on plate. Drizzle with pesto.

## Mini Cheese Balls On Pretzel Sticks

*Makes 8-10 little cheese balls, perfect for sharing with a friend*

8 oz cream cheese, softened

1 tablespoon mayonnaise

2 tablespoons minced green onion

1/2 – 3/4 cup grated parmesan, Swiss, or cheddar cheese

1/2 teaspoon garlic powder

small pretzel sticks

*Toppings :* (choose one or more)

chopped chives or parsley

bacon bits

chopped nuts

minced dried fruit

Mash together first five ingredients. Form into small balls with your hands. Roll in a topping of your choice---or mix it up  Stick a small pretzel stick in each. Chill at least an hour.

## ***Desserts and Sweets On A Stick***

*Of course kids need to eat a variety of foods, but there's nothing wrong with an occasional treat Some are wholesome enough for a side dish*

### **Fruit On A Stick ( and dip )**

*The dip sounds terrible. Try it anyway---it's addictive*

Fresh fruits: banana, apples, kiwi, grapes, melons, berries, pears, mango, stone fruits, pineapple, papaya , etc

1 cup sour cream

2 tablespoons brown sugar

Cut fruits into cubes, about the size of a grape. Thread on bamboo skewers.

Mix 1 sour cream and brown sugar. Serve skewers with the dip.

## Hand Pies On A Stick !

*Just right for a picnic or lunch box  Try the banana filling, or use any flavor jam*

Amazing Pie Crust dough (*see Empanadas On A Stick recipe*)

1 banana

8 ounces cream cheese

4 tablespoons confectioner's sugar

**Glaze**: 1 cup confectioner's sugar

few drops milk

few drops lemon juice

Preheat oven to 375 degrees

Mash banana with cream cheese and 4 tablespoons confectioner's sugar. Set aside. Roll out Amazing Pie Crust 1/4 inch thick.  Cut out 2 inch circles.  Place on parchment covered baking sheet. Set soaked craft stick on dough. Drop heaping teaspoon of banana filling in center of circle. Cover with second circle. Crimp edges firmly to seal. Cut tiny slit for steam to escape. Bake until just golden.

Mix Glaze, adding a few drops of liquid at a time, until just thin enough to drip off a fork, and smooth.  Drizzle glaze, using a fork, over each baked pie. Let set a few minutes, if you can wait that long!

## Cinnamon Snails On A Stick

*These are tiny, so use toothpicks or cut bamboo skewers in thirds. Any leftover **Amazing Pie Crust** recipe is great for these*

Roll out pie crust. Sprinkle with cinnamon and sugar, pressing lightly. Roll up, pinching edge to seal. Carefully cut into 1 inch slices. Place each slice on a skewer or toothpicks bake at 350 degrees until golden.

## Apple Wedges on A Stick

*A quick snack with endless variations Try peanut butter instead of frosting for a change*

Tart apples

prepared frosting ( any flavor; chocolate or white is good)

toppings:   graham cracker crumbs,  sprinkles, chocolate chips, mini marshmallows,  gummy candies,  chocolate covered candies, chopped nuts, coconut,  diced dry fruit, crushed cookies, etc.

Cut apples into wedges, and remove seeds.  Put on lollipop sticks. Smear   prepared frosting partway down each wedge.  Roll in topping of your choice

## Stuffed Strawberries On A Stick

*This may become your all-time favorite summertime dessert!*

2 lbs strawberries, chilled

8oz cream cheese, softened

2 teaspoons vanilla extract

3/4 cup powdered sugar

1/2 c. semi sweet chocolate chips

Wash and dry berries. Remove leaves, cutting a slight notch into the top of each berry. Beat cream cheese, vanilla, and powdered sugar together until smooth. Use an icing tip (or zip type bag with corner cut off) to squirt a bit of the cream cheese mixture onto the top of each strawberry. Insert craft or lollipop stick into each. Chill 15 minutes. Melt chocolate in microwave just until glossy, then stir to smooth. With a fork, drizzle a little chocolate across each berry. Chill.

## Chocolate Chip Cake Mix Cookies On A Stick !

*These are so easy, a child might not need much adult help at all You could use pretty much any drop-type cookie recipe to make wonderful cookies on a stick*

1 box yellow cake mix

1/2 cup oil OR butter or margarine, softened

2 tablespoons milk

1 egg

1 teaspoon vanilla

1 cup semisweet chocolate chips

1/2 cup chopped nuts, optional

Preheat oven to 350 degrees. Beat cake mix, butter, egg, and vanilla until combined. Stir in chocolate chips and nuts.

Drop dough by heaping teaspoons 2 inches apart on ungreased cookie sheets. Add craft stick.

Bake cookies 8-10 minutes, until edges are set and cookies are very light golden. Cool 1 minute; remove from cookie sheets to cooling rack.

## S'mores Cookies On A Stick

*For wintery days when you have a summer's craving. Cookies are fun in any form, but even better on a stick!*

3/4 cup graham crackers, crushed

2 cups flour

1/2 teaspoon baking soda

1/ 2 teaspoon salt

2 sticks butter, softened

1/4 cup brown sugar

1/2 cup sugar

1 egg

1 teaspoon vanilla extract

Chocolate candy bar, broken into pieces, OR chocolate chips

mini marshmallows , cut in half (use wet scissors)

Preheat oven to 375 degrees. Crush graham crackers thoroughly. Combine with flour, baking soda, and salt. Set aside. In another bowl, beat butter, sugars, egg, and vanilla until smooth. Combine both mixtures.

Form dough into 1 inch balls. Place on pan, and insert stick. Bake 8 minutes. Remove pan from oven. Carefully dot cookies with mini marshmallows and chocolate. Bake 3-4 more minutes, until the marshmallows began to melt. Remove from pan to cool.

## Jammy Cookies On A Stick

*Easy, and there's a surprise bite inside Next time, place a chocolate mint patty in place of the jam*

1 cup butter, softened

1 egg

3 ounces softened cream cheese

1 cup white sugar

1 teaspoon vanilla

1/2 teaspoon almond or lemon extract

3 cups flour

jam, any flavor

colored sugar

Beat butter, cream cheese and egg until creamy. Add sugar and extracts. Mix in flour gradually. Chill dough at least one hour.

Preheat oven to 375 degrees. Roll out dough on a lightly floured board about 1/8th inch thick. Cut with cookie cutter or glass. Transfer to baking sheet. Lay craft stick or coffee stirrer on dough. Drop scant teaspoon jam onto center of dough. Place another cut out on top, and press edges lightly to seal. Sprinkle with colored sugar. Bake 7 to 10 minutes, until edges are just golden. Cool on pan one minute before transferring to rack.

## Hot Cocoa On A Stick

*Stirred into a cup of hot milk, these fun sticks make wonderfully rich hot cocoa, with floating marshmallows The fudgy sticks are also delicious, eaten plain.*

mini marshmallows

1 bag (12 oz.) milk chocolate chips (or semi-sweet, or peanut butter flavor, or white chips; up to you!)

1 can sweetened condensed milk (NOT evaporated!)

1 tsp. vanilla

Skewer mini marshmallows on coffee stirrers, 4-8 per stick, bunched at one end to allow for stirring.

Melt the chocolate chips in a microwave, or double boiler, just until glossy. Stir to smooth out lumps. Add sweetened condensed milk and vanilla, stirring quickly until well blended. Dip and roll marshmallow end of stick in fudge to coat completely, then set on waxed paper. If you wish, rewarm fudge mixture and add a second coat to marshmallows. Wrap and chill to keep. To make hot cocoa, stir one stick in mug of hot milk.

## Itty Bitty Nutty Grapes On A Stick!

*You don't love nuts? Crushed pretzels or cookies are equally delicious*

grapes, washed and dried.

Caramel ice cream sauce

chopped nuts

Place one or two grapes on each toothpick. Dip halfway in caramel sauce, then roll in chopped nuts.

## Ice Cream Potatoes On A Stick!

*These make-ahead desserts look like little baked potatoes, with "sour cream "dipping sauce. Add green sprinkles for "chives", if you wish*

Ice cream (any flavor; light color looks best)

hot cocoa powder, or baking cocoa

marshmallow crème

Working quickly, form irregular blobs of ice cream, about 1/4 cup each, with your hands. Roll the blobs in cocoa to coat. Insert a craft stick. Freeze on waxed paper until firm. Serve with marshmallow crème for dipping.

## Frozen Bananas On A Stick

*Endless variations here Use other fruits, such as kiwi, peaches, grapes, or pineapple. Substitute thick Greek-style yogurt or nutella for the chocolate, and mix up the toppings any way you like You don't even have to freeze the fruit, but it's wonderful that way*

bananas, or other fruits, patted dry

milk chocolate chips

coconut, sprinkles, chopped nuts, crushed cookies, other toppings

Cut bananas in half. Add a stick to the end. Melt chocolate chips in microwave until glossy, and stir until smooth. Dip and smear chocolate over the fruit. Roll in topping of your choice, or leave plain. Freeze at least one hour.

*I hope you feel inspired to try these recipes, and make up your own. If you have enjoyed this book, or learned anything at all, please take a few moments to leave a <u>positive review. Five-star reviews</u> mean so much to authors---our livelihood depends on positive feedback You can even be anonymous if you prefer. And please take time to read my other books. You'll enjoy them. Thanks very much!*

## Quick and Clever Kid's Crafts

## by Deb Graham

## ©All Rights Reserved 2016

Suggested Craft Box Materials ..................................... 130
    For easier clean up: ........................................... 135
    Bird Feeders ...................................................... 135
    Candle Craft ...................................................... 137
    Ornaments ........................................................ 139
    **Cinnamon Ornaments** ................................... 139
    **Craft Stick Reindeer** ...................................... 140
    **Candy Cane Ornaments** ............................... 140
    **Playclay Ornaments** ..................................... 141
    **Icicles** ............................................................ 142
    **Clear Glass Ball Ornaments** ......................... 142
    Plaster Projects ................................................ 143
    **Lemon Plaster Cast Desk Bowl** .................... 144
    **Plaster Hand Casts** ...................................... 145
    **Beach Feet** ................................................... 145
    **Plaster Ladybugs Pins (or magnets)** ............ 146
    Beanbags .......................................................... 147
    **Mice Bean Bags** ........................................... 147
    **Generic Beanbags** ....................................... 147
    Peanut People .................................................. 148
    **Peanut People** .............................................. 148
    **Peanut Baby** ................................................. 148
    **Peanut Baby #2** ............................................ 149
    Paper Craft ........................................................ 149
    **Tissue Paper Butterflies** ............................... 149
    **House of Cards** ............................................ 150

Note Cards .................................................................. 151
**Sandpaper Note Cards** .............................................. 151
**Pop Up Cards** ............................................................ 152
**Thumbkins** ................................................................. 152
**Straw Painted Note Cards** ........................................ 153
**Leaf Rubbing Cards** .................................................. 153
Pompom Buddies ........................................................ 154
**PomPom Buddies** ..................................................... 154
**Footed Buddy** ........................................................... 154
**Pompom Octopus** ..................................................... 155
**Pompom Bat** ............................................................. 155
**Pompom Spiders** ...................................................... 155
Food Crafts ................................................................. 155
**Pasta Doodling** ......................................................... 155
**Mosaics** .................................................................... 156
**Popcorn Critters** ....................................................... 156
*Edible* **Peanut Butter Play Dough** .......................... 157
Clothespins, Pencils, and Paper Clips ....................... 158
**Tulip Clothespins** ..................................................... 158
**Fancy Paperclips** ..................................................... 158
**Paper Pencils** ........................................................... 159
Flower Pots ................................................................. 159
**Leaf Flower Pot** ........................................................ 159
**Fancy Patches Flower Pot** ....................................... 160
**Lacy Flower Pot** ....................................................... 160
Jewelry ........................................................................ 161

**Rolled beads** ................................................. 161
**Cookie Pendants** ........................................... 161
**Countertop Necklace** ..................................... 161
**Bangle Bracelet** ............................................. 162
Soap Crafts ...................................................... 162
**Soap With A Surprise Inside** ......................... 162
**Painted Soap** ................................................. 163
Puppets ............................................................ 164
**Lost Sock Puppets** ........................................ 164
**Wooden Spoon Puppets** ............................... 164
**Finger Puppets** .............................................. 165
Felt Hand Puppets ........................................... 166
Tee Shirt Art ..................................................... 166
**Vegetable Print Shirts** ................................... 166
**Masking Tape Shirts** ..................................... 167
Centerpieces .................................................... 168
**Frost on the Pumpkins** .................................. 168
**Canning Jar Lights** ........................................ 169
Paint Crafts ...................................................... 169
**String Stamps** ............................................... 169
**Lids and Cups Painting** ................................. 170
**Mosaic Dot Painting** ...................................... 170
**Spray Painted Spider Webs** ......................... 171
**Pie Pan Painting** ............................................ 172
**Night Sky Star Paper** .................................... 172
**Toothbrush Screen Painting** ......................... 173

Make Your Own Book ................................................. 173
**Your Own Amazing Book** ........................................ 173
Other Crafts ............................................................ 176
**Juice Lid Magnets** ................................................. 176
**Poetry Rocks** ....................................................... 176
**Balloon Flip Flops** ................................................ 177
**Basket Weaving** ................................................... 177
**Egg Head Pets** ..................................................... 177
**Tin Punching** ....................................................... 178
**Snazzy Button Covers** ........................................... 178
**Ironed Leaves** ...................................................... 179
**Shell Frames** ....................................................... 179
SWAPS ................................................................... 181
**Plaster Ladybugs** ................................................. 181
**Teepee** ............................................................... 182
**Bandage** ............................................................. 182
**Ice Cream Cone** ................................................... 183
**Gingerbread Cookie** .............................................. 183
**Alphabet Messages** .............................................. 184
**Beach Find Pals** ................................................... 184
**S'mores** .............................................................. 184
**Peanut People** ..................................................... 184
**Kites** .................................................................. 185
**Bedroll** ............................................................... 185
**Snowman** ........................................................... 185
**CD** .................................................................... 186

Go Fish ..........................................................................186

Sundae ..........................................................................186

Frying Pan ....................................................................186

Pennants ......................................................................187

Real Book ....................................................................187

Flowerpot ....................................................................187

Sit Upon ......................................................................187

Peas in a Pod ..............................................................188

Biffy Paper ..................................................................188

Bat ................................................................................188

Ants On A Log ............................................................189

Caterpillar ..................................................................189

Flip Flop Swap ..........................................................189

Campfire ....................................................................189

Pompom Octopus ......................................................190

Pompom Spiders ......................................................190

BONUS SECTION: Recipes..........................................190

Bread Modeling Dough ..............................................191

Bubbles ......................................................................191

Drink Mix Play Dough ................................................191

One Day Play Dough ................................................192

Awesome Sawdust Clay ............................................193

Sidewalk Chalk ..........................................................193

Cornstarch OooGoo ..................................................193

A SHAMELESS PLEA: ....................................................195

Easy, quality craft projects for children, classes, and scout groups, plus a bonus book of SWAPS

Bored kids? Sick child who won't rest? Whining children when the rain just won't quit? A sudden sleep over? Called upon to lead the troop this week? Need a project the whole classroom can do? This book in your hands is the answer to what to do when there's nothing to do. It's loaded with easy crafts with impressive results that any child can handle with minimal help. In fact the less help-- the better Adults will also find interesting projects here.

This book is TWO books in one The first section is on crafts, and the second on Swaps, little artwork- on- pins. Feel free to adapt any techniques that grab your attention in any fashion

*What do I know about Crafting?*

I'm a mom, and a grandmother. I was a Girl Scout and leader for ten years, including four summers leading at a Girl Scout day camp. I also served a couple of three year stints as a Cub Scout den mother, and several years at Cub Scout Camp. I've led the children's program in our Church for two 3-year bouts. On top of that, I live in the Pacific Northwest, where rainy days –no, weeks -- are the norm. I believe a bored child is an unhappy child, and no one wants to be around a grumpy kid Keep a kid busy, and they'll be much more fun to be around. I simply can't abide whining; it goes right through me, and makes me want to send the offender to clean a closet or some other awful chore. Better to break out the craft supply box

In a world where many children are electronically addicted, it's even more important to foster creative play and encourage imagination and inventiveness at every possible turn. So much of what children do see is non-interactive; they click a mouse or press a button, and something happens on a flat screen in front of them. Where's the fun in that?

Compare that to the genuine satisfaction that comes from a child exclaiming, "I made it *myself!*" It's a pleasure to watch a child faced with a pile of materials, suddenly break into creativity. In a group setting, the creativity that surfaces when given the same materials is amazing. That sense of accomplishment will last a lifetime. It's also tempting to rush a child, but adults need to keep an eye on the goal.

Let the child lead An adult should be nearby, in case help is needed to hold that part while glue is applied or to explain how to make a particular fold. Other than that, get out of the way A child needs to be free to make the project, not to copy an adult's work. The goal is creative play, and perhaps learning a new skill on the way. It is not to quickly make mass produced perfection Sometimes a child will make a nice little dough bird. Other times, they will be very content to spend 20 minutes simply squishing the dough, over and over. Both are valuable. This is ART and art takes time.

Be very careful not to squash budding artists, by fixing or straightening the end result. Yes, it may not be perfect in your eyes, but who put you in charge? In "fixing" a project, you very clearly teach a child that their effort is Not Good

Enough. That's a terrible lesson. Much better to give free rein, with the understanding that you have full faith in their ability to make something wonderful and they can clean up any messes later on.

There are life skills to be learned here, well beyond passing a dreary afternoon. The ability to think, to plan a project, to figure out new ways to use materials, to play with color and shapes and visualize the end result, to follow directions and then expand upon them, to care for one's materials and keep them somewhat organized, are all important skills. That doesn't even take into account the ongoing development of fine motor skills and hand-eye coordination, and the pure pleasure that comes from playing with tactile materials.

Teaching your child to care for materials will not crush their spirit of creativity. Rinsing out paintbrushes, not pounding markers, standing the glue upright so it will not spill, learning to cut pieces from the edge of paper, not the center, and so on will allow for more projects later Just be sure you are curbing disorder, not imagination.

Craft projects for kids are way more important that you may think at first glance!

I have assembled some tried-and true projects for you here. Some I recall doing when I was a six year old, others I have taught my own children and grandchildren, many more I have used in troop or den or Church class settings and at camp. All are inexpensive, because frugality is another important life lesson..

Many of the required materials are things you may already have around the house. Others are things found in any well-stocked craft supply box. You'll find, as you begin doing crafts with your kids, that your mindset will change. On your way to the recycling bin, you may look at that "trash" through new eyes; can it be reused, or turned into a wonderful project? What will result if you hand it to a child, instead of the trash bin?

Most of these crafts can be made outdoors, in a camp setting, with a group, or classroom setting, or indoors with one bored child on a rainy day. I suggest making them as described the first time, then modify as you see fit Be sure to praise creative effort along the way. The child is always more important than the result

## *Suggested Craft Box Materials*

*Try to have quality materials at hand. It's frustrating to try to make an art project with runny glue, crumbling crayons, or paintbrushes that shed. Don't make a big production out of acquiring these items Gather them as needed, gradually, saving leftover bits for future projects. To begin, you might look around the house, at yard sales, and at dollar stores for items that look like they have potential.*

old magazines with colorful photos

thick white craft glue

low temperature glue gun and glue sticks

glue sticks for paper

pipe cleaners ( the fuzzy wire chenille sticks)

fabric scraps

felt sheets

craft foam sheets ( like funfoam, comes in many colors, easily cut)

sandpaper

plastic spoons and knives

paper plates

stapler

feathers

clean dry yogurt containers, with lids

ribbons, both fabric and gift-wrap type

glitter

magnets

cotton balls

paint brushes, preferably soft, varying widths

foam paint brushes for larger projects

little bottles for storing tiny items –prescription bottles are great

lace scraps

plastic drinking straws

newsprint roll ends (from local newspaper printing office; often free or cheap)

brown kraft paper (comes on a roll)

old toothbrushes

colored tissue paper

yarn

string and twine

wooden craft sticks; popsicle sticks or tongue depressors

wax and old candles

construction paper

card stock paper

scrapbook paper

gift wrapping paper

ink pads

small jars (baby food, spice jars, etc)

simple stencil set

egg cartons

dry beans and large seeds

dry pasta in fun shapes

needles and thread for sewing

smooth rocks

paper sacks of all sizes, especially lunch sacks

seashells

scissors, and perhaps scissors with designed blades

craft knife, like X-Acto brand

mismatched socks

cardboard from sturdy box

markers (thick, thin, permanent, washable)

crayons ---get good quality, they last a long time

stickers

chalk and sidewalk chalk

googly eyes ( plastic craft eyes, sold in bags and varying sizes at craft stores)

pompoms of various sizes and colors

an old blow dryer to speed up paint drying

wire

buttons

beads of various sizes and shapes; watch for old jewelry, too

aluminum foil

waxed paper

ruler

masking tape and clear tape

pencils

colored pencils

dry plaster of Paris

acrylic paints; in little bottles or tubes from craft stores

tempera paints; dry version costs much less

watercolors set

## For easier clean up:

smock (man's old button down shirt; worn backwards)

plastic disposable table cover; easy to wrap up mess and all at the end of the project

**best yet**: crafts done outdoors require less clean up. So what if the water spills?

Consider providing a place for items to dry, as well as be displayed. A simple string with clothespins on a wall does just fine.

## Bird Feeders

### Heart Bird Seed Feeder

Flat wooden heart cut out shape

white glue

birdseed

1/4 inch ribbon (approx. 6 inches)

Glue ribbon to the heart to form a loop hanger. Cover the wooden heart completely in glue (not dripping) and then place the heart in a bowl of bird seed. Cover the heart with the birdseed, patting to make sure no bare spots are left. Let the glue dry. Hang heart in a tree or where birds have easy access to it.

### Orange Peel Bird Feeder

Scoop out the pulp from half of an *orange,* leaving peel intact. Punch three holes about 1/ 4" down from the top, spacing to form a rough triangle. String a 12-15 " ***yarn*** through each hole and tie together at the top. Adjust length depending on where it will be hung. Mix **peanut butter and**

**birdseed** or **suet and birdseed,** and fill the cavity. Hang outside for birds to enjoy.

## Birdseed Pinecones

Cover a fist-sized **pinecone** with **peanut butter**. Roll in **birdseed** or **sunflower seeds** to cover. Add a **string loop,** and hang for birds to enjoy

## **Candle Craft**

### Sand Candles

Make a fist-sized (or slightly larger) indentation in **clean damp sand,** either on the beach or in a bucket. Form *three shallow feet with your finger in bottom of indentation. Add **seashells or small pretty rocks**, remembering that the side facing down will show when candle is complete. Set one, two, or three **wicks** in place. Carefully melt **wax** in a double boiler made of a can set in simmering water. Pour wax into sand, adding more to level as it cools. Cool overnight, then brush sand off sides.

*Three legs are always more stable than four*

## Ice Candles

*I remember making these as a brownie, decades ago*
*They're just as enjoyable now*

pint or quart sized paper milk carton, washed and dry

ice

wax

wick

Arrange broken **ice cubes** or large crushed ice in a **paper milk carton.** Melt **wax** in an empty can set in simmering water. Pour wax over ice, turning carton to cover ice. Let set. Pour off water, then peel off paper carton. Heat ice pick until hot enough to insert in ice, to the bottom. Poke **wick** in wax. Decorate with **glitter, beads, or dried flowers**. *Decorative only.*

## Pressed Flower Candles

*Using ready-made candles makes this project a snap, plus leaves room for creativity in decorating*

Melt white **wax** in a double boiler. Using a disposable paintbrush, brush the wax onto a **votive, pillar candle or taper**. Working quickly, press **pressed flowers and leaves** onto candle. Cool. These make nice gifts

## Ornaments

### Cinnamon Ornaments

1 cup applesauce

6 oz cinnamon

1/3 cup white glue

Mix together to form a ball. Refrigerate 30 minutes .Sprinkle extra cinnamon on waxed paper and roll out to ¼ inch thickness. Cut with cookie cutters. Use straw to form hole in top. Let air-dry for about 2 days. May be decorated with sequins, jewels, yarn, lace, etc.

### Craft Stick Reindeer

3 wooden craft sticks

2 googly eyes
1 1/4 inch red pompom
Glue
6 inches ribbon for hanger

Make a capital letter "A" with the sticks. Glue at the top and on the crossbar of the "A". Then turn the "A" upside down so the point is on the bottom. This will be the nose. Glue the red pompom onto the point. Glue the eyes on the cross bar. Glue the ribbon onto the back of the "antlers" to hang.

### Candy Cane Ornaments

Cut a **white pipe cleaner** into 4 inch lengths. Alternate **red and white plastic tri-beads**. Bend the top part down enough to make it look like a candy cane. **Glue** the ends so the beads don't come off.

## Playclay Ornaments

1 lb box *baking soda*

1 cup *corn starch*

1 cup cold *water.*

Stir together 1 lb box **baking soda** and 1 cup **corn starch** in saucepan. Add 1 cup cold **water.** Cook over medium heat, stirring constantly, until mixture reaches consistency of moist mashed potatoes (approximately 10-15 minutes.) Remove and put on a plate. Cover with a damp cloth. When cool enough to handle, knead until smooth. Roll out and cut with cookie cutters or form freehand shapes. Try to make shapes no more than 3 /4" thick. When sticking one piece to another, moisten where the pieces are joined. Allow to dry, then paint and decorate.

## Icicles

*These are quick, easy and pretty Beads are sold in labeled packages in craft stores, and the bags contain enough for several icicles.*

Cut a **silver pipe cleaner** in half and turn up the end slightly so that the beads won't fall off. Put on **four 6mm faceted beads, four 8mm faceted beads, four tri beads, four small paddle wheel (sunburst) beads, then four large clear paddle wheel beads**. Make a loop at the top with the rest of the pipe cleaner and tie on **string or ribbon for** hanger.

### Clear Glass Ball Ornaments

Make a sketch or use a **clipart** of any scene you like; perhaps a troop crest or a patch, an animal, a Nativity scene, with a circle around it, a bit smaller than the diameter of a **clear glass round Christmas ornament**. Copy several onto a page, if multiples are desired. Have a copy center copy designs onto an **overhead projector plastic sheet.** Cut out the circle. Remove the top from the ornament. Roll the plastic design around a **pencil,** then slide into the ornament, right side up. Remove pencil. The plastic will pop out flat. Replace top of ornament. Add a **ribbon or bow.**

### Light Bulb Reindeer

*Great way to recycle used light bulbs*

Paint a **light bulb** gold or brown, including the metal base, using **acrylic paint**. Let dry. Turn base-side up. Wrap a **brown pipe cleaner** around base (which is now the top) and twist to secure, leaving ends free. Cut another pipe cleaner in half. Bend one half to form antlers on one side, then repeat on other pip cleaner. Glue on **googly eyes** and a **red pompom** near the bottom of the bulb for a nose.

## Plaster Projects

*Plaster of Paris is a great material, full of potential, and you can even use scraps for drawing on sidewalks Be sure to protect indoor surfaces, and wash hands after use.*

## Lemon Plaster Cast Desk Bowl

*Seems children are always looking for a gift for a parent, friend, teacher, and so on This makes a little bowl, perfect for a desk, just right for paperclips, and rubber bands, and other small treasures. May use baseball, toy cars, acorn squash, etc instead of lemon. The hardest part is waiting for it to set up*

Plaster of Paris

water

half gallon milk carton, cut to 3" tall

large lemon

acrylic paint

 Mix plaster of Paris as directed on package, enough to fill carton mold 3/4ths full. Working quickly, press lemon halfway into plaster. Wait 4 minutes, then carefully remove lemon. The indentation makes the bowl part. Let plaster dry thoroughly. Peel off paper mold. Paint with acrylic paints. This looks especially nice with the lemon part a different color than the base part.

## Plaster Hand Casts

*These are a fun group project; sing as the plaster cures. They are a great way to look back years later to see how much a child's hand has grown. I still have the one I made at camp when I was six. It looks like a seashell.*

Mix **plaster of Paris** as directed on package. Hold hands together in a slightly overlapped cup shape. Have another person pour plaster into tightly cupped hands. Hold hands together, without wiggling, until plaster warms up and begins to cool. Carefully move fingers and set shape aside to dry. Can be painted or decorated with markers.

## Beach Feet

*A beach is ideal for this project. Use a shallow box of sand if damp sand is not available. At the beach, choose the hard packed sand not far from the waterline.*

Press both **bare feet** into the **sand,** making prints about 2" deep. Mix **plaster of Paris** according to package directions---the water is right there  Gently pour the plaster into each footprint. If you want a hanger, tie a knot into a 4" piece of **string** to form a loop, for each footprint. Press knot into plaster. Let harden 15 minutes. Gently pull up prints, and set to dry.

## Plaster Ladybugs Pins (or magnets)

*These are so cute and easy, you'll want to make a lot at once  Each will have its own personality, as varying dots are added.*

 Line up a series of **plastic spoons**, bowl side up, on a protected surface. Mix **plaster of Paris** as directed on package. Fill each spoon with plaster. Tap to level. Let dry thoroughly.  Pop plaster out, and decorate to resemble lady bug, using **paint or markers.**

To make a pin, carefully stand an open safety pin in the wet plaster, "head side" down, leaving pointy side free. Or glue a magnet on the flat side when dry.

# Beanbags

## Mice Bean Bags

Cut two **felt** ovals, about 3 X 4 inches. Sew around edge, but before closing, pour in ½ **cup dry beans or corn**. Stitch closed. Sew on round felt ears, and add felt nose, eyes, and yarn tail.

## Generic Beanbags

*These have endless uses, and are just waiting for some inspiration  Make up a tossing game, make a car fleet, build a family, on and on*

Sew together two pieces of **felt**, cut into matching shapes, such as circles, or squares. About 3 X4 inches is a good size. Leave an opening about 2" long. Carefully pour in **dry beans or corn,** leaving enough space for the beanbag to be floppy. Sew opening closed. **Glue** on whatever is needed: eyes, hair, faces, wheels, etc, and let dry.

## Peanut People

***Unshelled peanuts*** come in a wide variety of shapes, just like people Draw on faces with markers, then glue on bits of fabric to add clothes, hats, scarves, capes. Add yarn or embroidery thread hair. Bits of cotton balls make beards.

## Peanut Baby

Glue **googly eyes** to an in-the-shell **peanut.** Add a triangle of **white felt** for a diaper.

## Peanut Baby #2

Wrap u**nshelled peanut** in 2" square of ***flannel***, like a baby blanket (set on corner, fold up bottom, side, side). Glue to hold. Draw on eyes with thin marker.

## Paper Craft

### Tissue Paper Butterflies

*These cheery little butterflies can be hung anywhere Even little fingers can make beautiful ones, with little or no help. Once you master the concept, make fancier ones by layering tissue paper of different colors, pulling apart layers gently. These are easily glued to spring type clothespins, making curtain-hanging even easier.*

Cut **tissue paper** into an oval, about 5" by 3 1/2 inches. Fold a **pipe cleaner** in half. Fan fold just the center of the paper, and wrap with the pipe cleaner, bending ends to form antennae.

## House of Cards

*This is a fun activity to play in the car on a long drive. The cards lock together with slits, so it is much more stable than an ordinary card house*

Find a **deck of discarded playing cards.** Using a scissor, make a 1 inch slit in the top, bottom and both sides of each card, roughly centered, one at a time. Join the cards together by interlocking the slits to build towers, bridges, etc.

You could also make your own cards by tracing a shape onto poster board, then cutting out and adding slits. Cards are rectangles, but you can also use circles, triangles or whatever you choose, so long as they have slits to interlock. Store in envelope for another day's play.

## Note Cards

*Don't let note-writing become a lost art Encourage children to write thank you notes, get well cards, make their own birthday cards, etc. Everyone enjoys mail, and sending a card you made yourself is a double pleasure*

## Sandpaper Note Cards

Color a simple design onto **sandpaper,** using vibrant **crayons** and pressing hard to get as much wax onto the sandpaper as possible. Layer **newspaper** on a towel-covered table. Place the sandpaper on newspaper, crayon side up. Cover with **cardstock note card**. Iron on top of the cardstock, just until wax melts. Don't go for any detailed design; simple shapes such as trees, apples, stars work best.

## Pop Up Cards

*These are very easy, versatile, and a nice change for any occasion requiring a card Half of a standard 8.5" X 11 paper fits an 'invitation' size envelope perfectly.*

Start with **cardstock,** a bit narrower than an **envelope** and twice as tall. Fold in half to make a card. On the creased side, cut two slits, about 1.5 inches apart and about an inch deep. Open the card, and push the cut flap through, then pinch to crease. It will look like a little step inside. Set the card aside. Make a design on a separate paper, maybe a word or a picture, and cut it out. Glue the smaller piece to the _front_ of the "step" on the vertical part. A **glue stick** works well. Let dry completely, write a cheery message, and you're done

## Straw Painted Note Cards

*Remember to take breaks to breathe normally. This is so much fun, that it's easy to get light-headed just from blowing and not inhaling enough*

Cut **cardstock** in half, and fold to make a card. On the front panel, drop a few drips of **tempera paint or India ink.** Holding a **drinking straw** close to paint, but not touching, blow and direct the paint into ever thinner lines. If you wish to add another color, let first one dry. Great for thank you notes

## Thumbkins

*These one-of-a-kind prints make charming note cards, gift tags, or pictures. Prevent smears by pausing to wipe your hands with a baby wipe, or wash your hands after making the thumbprint, then resume project.*

Press your thumb into an **ink pad,** and position your thumb print on **paper or blank card.** Using thin **markers,** add details, such as faces, antlers, feet, stick figure type arms and legs, ears, fins, tails, etc, to create animals or people.

## Leaf Rubbing Cards

*Choose fresh leaves; dried ones will crumble. Besides leaves, what else can you rub?*

Cut **cardstock** sheet in half, then fold to form card. Place a **leaf** or two inside the card, vein side up. Fold the card closed. Use a **colored pencil or crayon** to rub over the leaf so the design shows on the cover of the card.

## Pompom Buddies

**PomPom Buddies**

*Pompoms come on various sizes and colors. The easiest buddies have just googly eyes glued on, but let the imagination go Finished buddies can be glued to hair clips, notes, jars, boxes, gift tags-- endless possibilities What other critters come to mind?*

### Footed Buddy
Glue a heart shaped piece of **felt** onto a **pompom**, to make feet. Add **eyes**, hair, and details as desired.

## Pompom Octopus

Braid 4 lengths of *yarn*, and glue on the bottom of pompom to make octopus arms.

## Pompom Bat

Cut wing shapes out of **black craft foam**. Glue a **black pompom** to center, add **googly eyes**.

## Pompom Spiders

Glue 4 long **black pipe cleaner** legs to the bottom of a **black pompom**. Bend pipe cleaner into spider's legs. Add **googly eyes** and a **string** to the top. Dry . Dangle, wait for screams.

# Food Crafts

## Pasta Doodling

Cook a handful of **spaghetti** until soft but not mushy. Drain, and rinse with cold water. Use the strands to make pictures on **dark construction paper**, cutting with butter knife as needed. The starch will make the pasta stick to the paper. If it gets too dry to adhere, mist very lightly with water in a plant mister.

To preserve the finished artwork, cover it with **waxed paper** and a heavy book until dry. The pasta will adhere even when it dries.

## Mosaics

*These can be stunning*

Set out a variety of dried foods: little pasta shapes, dried beans, seeds, popcorn, whatever else is available in the pantry. Smear white glue on small section of cardstock at a time, and fill in using the foodstuffs. Let dry before displaying.

## Popcorn Critters

*Use "mushroom" variety popcorn; it makes broader shapes, ideal for designing. This activity requires some dexterity, so it's recommended for older artists; toddlers will be frustrated. Each will be unique. Suggested starting point: poodles, of course*

Pop a small amount of **mushroom popcorn,** plus more for inevitable snacking of kernels that are not the shapes desired. **Markers** work best, but if you are careful not to soak the popcorn, **acrylic paint** can be used. Very carefully, decorate popcorn pieces to resemble a person or animal, gluing more together with small amounts of **craft glue** as needed. You can add eyes using **seed beads**, even a tiny **ribbon** if desired.

### *Edible*   Peanut Butter Play Dough

In a medium bowl, combine 2 cups **peanut butter**, 2 cups **powdered milk**, and 3 tablespoons **honey**. If too sticky, add more powdered milk, one tablespoon at a time. If desired, add chopped nuts or raisins to dough shapes . Sculpt, then snack

## Clothespins, Pencils, and Paper Clips

### Tulip Clothespins

*Fun to use for camp, or displaying art work at home. They're cute clamped onto a hat or vest, too. What other shapes come to mind?*

Cut stem, leaf, and tulip shape out of **craft foam**, just large enough to cover a spring type **clothespin. Glue** to a wooden **spring-type clothespin.** Let dry.

## Fancy Paperclips

*These are very simple, and pretty Make a bunch, arrange a few nicely on a card, and you have a fine gift for a mom or leader. Everyone needs paperclips!*

Cut a 5 inch length of **narrow fabric ribbon**, any color. Tie it in a lark's head\* knot through the top of a **large paperclip**. Secure with dab of **craft glue**. Let dry, then trim the tails about 2" long, at an angle.

*\*lark's head: fold ribbon in half, and pull looped end partway through the paperclip. Reaching through the loop, pull both <u>ends</u> of the ribbon through, and pull tight*

## Paper Pencils

Carefully roll a strip of pretty **wrapping paper** around a wooden **pencil** to measure size. Cut slightly wider, but not longer. Coat pencil lightly in **white glue**, and roll paper tightly around pencil, not covering eraser part. Let dry overnight. May be sharpened and used as any regular pencil.

## Flower Pots

### Leaf Flower Pot

Collect interesting **leaves**, that will fit onto a **terra cotta flower pot.** Paint the pot a base color (gold looks nice!) using **spray paint or acrylic paint**. Let dry. Brush **rubber cement** on back of leaf. Position on pot, and rub to adhere. Spray a light coat of contrasting color. Let dry. Peel off leaf. Rub off remaining rubber cement.

### Fancy Patches Flower Pot

Cut scraps of pretty *fabric* into 2" squares. Non-stretch is best. Brush **craft *glue*** onto section of a clean, dry terra *cotta flower pot.* If glue is too thick, thin with tiny bit of water. Press a square onto glue. Continue adding glue and squares until pot is covered, overlapping where needed. Brush entire surface with glue. It will dry clear and shiny, ready to fill with potting soil and a plant. Looks good with fabric flowers, too

## Lacy Flower Pot

Use same technique as above, except substitute cut *paper doilies* for fabric

## Jewelry

### Rolled beads

Cut colorful *magazine pages* into long narrow triangles, about two inches long and one inch at the wide end, tapering to a point at the other end. Roll paper around **skewers** or *toothpicks,* starting at wide end. Secure tip with *white glue.* Slide off skewer or toothpick, and make many more. Let dry completely before stringing. Great for necklaces!

### Cookie Pendants

Choose firm small **cookies**, such as animal crackers, fortune cookies, chocolate chip, oreos, ginger snaps, etc. Carefully brush off all crumbs. Coat all sides with clear or glitter **nail polish,** allowing to dry before coating back side. Use 2-3 coats to make it hard. Glue a small loop of **pipe cleaner** on the back, and string a **ribbon** through the loop to make a unique necklace.

## Countertop Necklace

Get free **countertop samples** from cabinet store. Paint front with acrylic paint, a simple design such as a flower or glue on pretty **wrapping paper.** Measure a ribbon length suitable for necklace, allowing room to slip over head. Run the **ribbon** through hole, tie in *lark's head knot.


*lark's head: fold ribbon in half, and pull looped end partway through the paperclip. Reaching through the loop, pull both ends of the ribbon through, and pull tight. For necklace, tie ends together.


## Bangle Bracelet

Measure child's wrist. Cut a length of **clear aquarium tube** 1" longer. Carefully fill with **beads, glitter, confetti,** etc. **Tape** ends together with clear tape.

## Soap Crafts

### Soap With A Surprise Inside

*A mold can be any small container, soap-sized, lined with plastic wrap. Clean dry yogurt containers work great, but see what else you can find. These are nice little gifts, and can even encourage a child to wash hands more often---they can't get the toy until the soap is used up*

Melt a block of **clear glycerin soap** in a double boiler or microwave. Place a **tiny toy** (car, necklace, ball, jacks, etc) in each **small mold**, then pour soap to fill mold, or to a good thickness if mold is too deep. Let harden, then pop out of mold. Wrap in clear plastic wrap.

## Painted Soap

*These make fun gifts---everyone uses soap The design lasts as long as the soap*

Paint a simple design on the flat surface of a **bar of soap** using **acrylic paint**. Dry. Melt **craft wax** or a white candle in a double boiler made of a clean dry tin can in a pot of simmering water. Use a disposable paintbrush to quickly coat the painted side of the soap. As the soap us used, the protective coating preserves the design.

**Alternative**: Cut picture from magazine to fit soap. Moisten flat side of soap, and press picture to adhere. Dry, then apply wax.

## Puppets

## Lost Sock Puppets

*At last, a use for the socks whose mates have wandered*

Use one **lonely sock** for each puppet. Lay flat, and line with **plastic wrap or waxed paper** to prevent glue seeping through sock. Use **craft glue** or **low-temp hot glue gun** Make face with **googly eyes and felt scraps**. Add **yarn** hair, **fabric** hats, a cape, whatever the sock wants for its new identity. Let dry, remove lining, and have a puppet show!

## Wooden Spoon Puppets

*Dollar stores often have several wooden cooking spoons in a pack, a frugal way to make several puppets*

Using **paint or markers**, make a face on the bowl part of **wooden spoons.** Let dry. Add **yarn** hair, and decorate with **ribbons or scraps of fabric**, tied or glued on. Let the show begin

## Finger Puppets

*These are so simple, your artists will make a whole crowd in an afternoon  They can be people, characters, animals, or adorable monsters. They're also nice to tuck into a Church bag or diaper bag to entertain squirmy little people*

Cut two pieces of **felt,** each about 3.5" tall and 2" wide. Slightly round the top corners.  Pin together, then sew around edges, leaving bottom open. You can run them up quickly on a sewing machine to jump-start the project, or hand stitch. Remove pin. Let the creativity begin  Glue on **googly eyes, yarn** hair, manes, bows, a fabric cape, on and on

## Felt Hand Puppets

*Suggestions: lions, bears, people, cats, rabbits*

Trace a rough outline a little larger than the child's hand to make a pattern, like a fat mitten. Cut two pieces of **felt**, for the front and back. Whipstitch by hand, or have an older child sew around sides and top with a sewing machine, leaving bottom open. Cut and glue on ears, if needed. Decorate with **googly eyes, yarn, ribbon,** and whatever seems best

# Tee Shirt Art

## Vegetable Print Shirts

*These turn out surprisingly beautiful, and you'll never look at a vegetable in the same way again While the creative juices are flowing, what else can you make? Cards, pictures, wall hanging?*

Use just about any **vegetable or fruit**. Leave as is, or cut flat to expose interior shape. If cut, let dry with cut side down on paper towels 5 minutes. Lay **tee shirt** out flat, and slip layer of flat **newspaper** inside so the paint will not bleed through. Pour some **fabric paint** onto **paper plate**. Carefully dip vegetable into paint, or dab some paint on with paintbrush, and practice making prints on paper. Once comfortable, paint directly on shirt. When dry, heat set according to paint instructions.

*Suggested :    Corn on the cob (roll or use sideways slice), citrus slices, broccoli (cut down center of "tree" part), turnip shapes, potatoes (can cut away excess flesh with paring knife), carrot slices or cubes,   celery (cut end makes  arcs) , apple halves (either direction. Sideways exposes a star!) pears, cauliflower*

## Masking Tape Shirts

*These are easy, and surprisingly nice They'd be a fun activity at a birthday party or sleepover*

masking tape

plain t shirt

acrylic paint

sponge

Using strips of **masking tape**, arrange a design on the front of a **light colored t shirt**. You can make a starburst, collar, simple words,, zigzags stripes, etc. Secure the tape against fabric. Dab **acrylic paint** lightly on the shirt with a **sponge**, taking care to paint over edges of the tape. Let dry, and remove tape to reveal design.

## Centerpieces

### Frost on the Pumpkins

*A classy and easy Autumn centerpiece*

Choose a nice smooth **pumpkin**, or use mini ones. Wash and dry. Using **white dimensional paint**, generously paint on snowflakes by making an X, then adding a third line through the center. Before paint dries, sprinkle with white or clear **glitte**r. Work quickly, adding more snowflakes and glitter before paint dries.

### Canning Jar Lights

*These make striking centerpieces, party lights, or nightlights Experiment with varying sizes of jars, and patterned tissue paper*

For each one, cut **colored tissue paper** to loosely fit into a **canning jar**. Place a **battery-operated tea light** in the bottom. Replace lid, or leave off. That's it

## Paint Crafts

## String Stamps

*These stamps can be used on paper, fabric or t shirts May as well make several at once.*

***Tip:*** *you may find it easier to hold the stamp if you glue a simple flap of cardboard on the back side of the square for a handle.*

Cut **corrugated cardboard** into 3" square. Draw a simple design on each, such as a squiggle or concentric swirl. Trace an even line of **craft glue**, following the design. Press a single strand of **thick twine** directly on the glue line. Let dry completely.

To use the stamp, pour a thin layer of **acrylic or fabric paint** into a paper plate. Dip the twine side of the stamp into the paint, then carefully apply to the project; card, t shirt, etc. Apply even pressure, then remove stamp. Stamp can probably be used 2-3 times before dipping in paint again. Beautiful

## Lids and Cups Painting

Pour a small amount of ***poster paint*** into a shallow container, such as a sturdy paper plate. Dip the rim of an empty yogurt cup into paint and then press onto ***paper*** to make circle prints. Use both top and bottom rims for a variation of size, overlapping designs. Sprinkle with **salt or glitter** before paint dries.

## Mosaic Dot Painting

Any shape or size **clear glass jar or bottle** will work well here  This is a children's project, but adults are easily drawn into this one as well.

Squirt a pea-size puddle of **acrylic craft paint** onto a **paper plate**. Dip  the head of a **straight pin** into the paint. Make a dot on the side of a clean glass jar. Make more dots, in a curved or straight line, without redipping the pin until the dots get too small. The dots will get progressively smaller.  Add more dots, and more colors, to make any design you wish

## Spray Painted Spider Webs

*This works best on windless days, often near dawn when large flat spider webs are abundant. It's easier with two people.*

Find a suitable **spider web**, and very carefully encourage the occupant to stand aside.  Carefully spray a thin mist of contrasting color **spray paint** across the web to wet it, but not enough to cause sagging. Working fast, have the second person position a **large sheet of paper or construction paper** behind the web, just touching the strands, scooping it so the web will stick to the paper.  Let dry.

## Pie Pan Painting

Cut plain **paper** to fit flat inside pie pan. Secure on back with tiny loop of tape. Drip several drops of **paint** onto paper, one or two colors at most. Add a few **marbles or a golf ball**. Swirl to make one-of-a-kind patterns

## Night Sky Star Paper

Draw white stars with **white crayon** on **white construction paper**, pressing down hard. Dilute **black poster paint** with a little water. Brush over the entire paper. Let dry. The stars shine through the black "sky!

## Toothbrush Screen Painting

Set a fairly flat *shape* onto a *paper or blank card.* Examples include a leaf, a paper cut out, coins, etc. Very lightly dip the bristles of an *old toothbrush* into *poster paint*. Holding a square of **window screen** over the paper, rub and flick the brush to release paint through the screen. Remove the item to reveal design.

## Make Your Own Book

### Your Own Amazing Book

*Once you grasp the general concept, you can make dozens of these handmade little treasures*

2 pieces cardboard, 6 1/2" by 9 1/4"

needle and thread, or sewing machine

non-stretchy fabric 16" X 12", pressed flat

paper

paper clips

ruler

white or craft glue

Cut the paper to measure 5 1/2" by 8 1/2". Add extra page; if you want 8 pages to write on, put in 4 papers for writing and 1 extra, or 5 total pages. Limit these books to just a few pages; they become unmanageable if too thick. Stack neatly, and fold in half, holding corners with paper clip. Sew down the center with machine or hand stitch. Set aside.

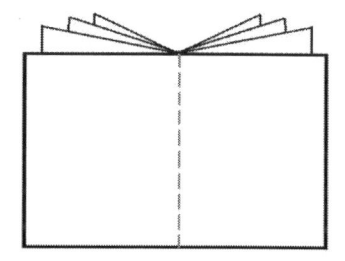

Lay out fabric, right side down. Set the cardboard on the fabric, leaving a border, and about ¼ inch between cardboard. Glue the cardboard down.

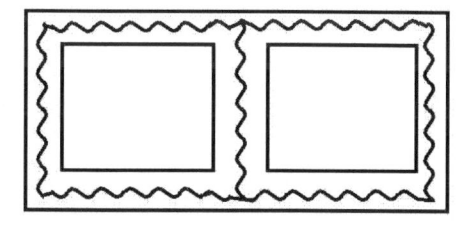

Fold the corners of the fabric in and glue down. Then fold in sides and neatly glue them to cardboard cover. Let dry.

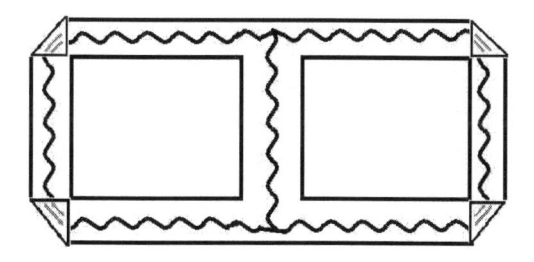

## Other Crafts

### Juice Lid Magnets

*Even very young hands can make these*

Wash and dry **metal juice can lids**. Trace cut outs from **scrapbook paper or wrapping paper. Glue** onto front of lid. Add **magnet** on the back.

### Poetry Rocks

Wash and dry a heap of small, smooth **pebbles,** approximately 1-3 inches in size. Write one word on each, using thin **marker**. Be careful to include all parts of speech Move words around to make up poetry or a story.

### Balloon Flip Flops

Tie a series of uninflated latex **balloons** close together on straps of plastic **flip flops** using a tight single knot, stretching to tighten. Easy, adorable

## Basket Weaving

Cut the bottom 4-5" off of a ***2 litre soda bottle.*** Cut uneven number of vertical slits all around, about ¾ inch apart, leaving one inch intact at top, and bottom , using craft knife. Weave ***strips of light fabric*** in and out, all around, pushing down as you go to fill in the slits. Tuck in stray ends.

## Egg Head Pets

*It's fun to make several at once, with different faces*

Carefully chip open a fresh **egg,** leaving a hole on the end of the eggshell about the size of a quarter. Rinse the shell and let dry. Decorate with a face, using **permanent markers or acrylic paints**, so the face won't run when you water the hair. Set in egg carton or small paper ring. Use a spoon to fill the shell with **potting soil,** then sprinkle a teaspoon or so of **grass seed** on top. Tamp gently. Moisten the soil, cover with **plastic wrap,** and set in a warm place to sprout. Seeds usually germinate in under a week. At this point, you can style hair into Mohawks or pigtails, and cut as desired with scissors. Water when the soil seems dry.

## Tin Punching

Draw a very simple outline of a design on a paper cut to fit inside a ***metal juice can lid***. Heart, smiley face, star, etc. Tape the paper to the lid. Place lid on scrap wood surface, or work on ground. Carefully tap ***nail*** with ***hammer*** to puncture evenly along the design. Remove paper to reveal dotted design. Add a ***ribbon*** through another hole at top to hang. Once you feel confident with technique, try a pie tin

## Shell Frames

*Gather frames from dollar stores, yard sales, or the back of Mom's closets, where unwanted ones seem to congregate.*

*Ideal for a beach trip photo, or a pretty gift.*

Arrange **seashells** and **small beach pebbles** on the frame, and glue in place, using thick craft glue, taking care to cover the frame while leaving the glass part visible. Let dry.

## Snazzy Button Covers

*Endless variety*

Cut bright **craft foam** into 2" shapes, such as a flower, animal, face, star, etc. Cut 1" slit in center. Carefully slip over buttoned buttons on front of any shirt. Remove before laundering

## Ironed Leaves

On a dry autumn day, gather **bright colored leaves**. They need to be fairly clean, and dry. Cut **waxed paper** twice as large as the leaf, and fold in half. Slip leaf between waxed paper. Under adult supervision, **iron** each leaf, taking care to seal the waxed paper around all sides. These are pretty hung in a window, or can be cut apart to make other projects

## *SWAPS*

Swaps are traditionally little pieces of handmade art "swapped" among Girl Scout troops when they meet another troop, as a tiny gift. They are often worn on hats or vests, or displayed on boards, the more the merrier  Swaps can represent a particular activity, such as camping, or an outing, such as bowling. A*ny tiny craft makes a fine swap* **Be sure to glue or otherwise attach a safety  pin on the back of every swap**  so it can be displayed or worn.

These clever little pieces of artwork also make great pins for moms to wear, or tiny gifts. Visiting a nursing home? Residents would probably appreciate a bright little gift. They're easy to make in assembly line fashion, making lots in a short time.  And of course, these ideas and techniques can be adapted to many other projects

### Teepee

Draw tiny designs on brown **kraft paper**. using **thin sticks** and **glue,** fashion tiny teepee. Add pin with glue

## Plaster Ladybugs

*These are so cute and easy, you'll want to make a lot at once*

e

Line up a series of **plastic spoons**, bowl side up, on a protected surface. Mix about a half cup of **plaster of Paris** as directed on package. Fill each spoon with plaster. Tap to level. Let dry thoroughly. Pop plaster out, and decorate to resemble lady bug, using **paint or markers.**

To make a pin, carefully stand an open safety pin in the **wet** plaster, "head side" down, leaving pointy side free.

## Bandage

Cut bandage shape of **pink craft foam, a narrow rectangle with rounded corners**. Glue **tan square** in center for pad. Add ink dots for bandage 'pad'

## Ice Cream Cone

Shape a circle of **kraft paper** into a cone, adding little lines for texture as desired with **a pen.** Glue 1-3 **pompoms** on top for ice cream.

### Gingerbread Cookie

Cut a small gingerbread man cookie shape out of **coarse sandpaper.** Add **crayon** eyes and glue on buttons down the front

### Reindeer or Moose Swap

See above. Turn the gingerbread shape upside down, so the feet are up. The feet become antlers; see? Add a face with eyes and a tiny pompom nose

### Alphabet Messages

**Glue** words of dry **alphabet pasta** on **craft foam** shapes, spelling out names, words, etc

### Beach Find Pals

Jazz up a tiny piece of **driftwood** with **googly eyes** and a **yarn** scarf. Glue a pin on the back

## S'mores

Make a s'more by layering square of **tan felt** (cracker), then **dark brown felt** (chocolate), wisp of **cotton ball** (marshmallow), and another tan square on top. **Glue** together, or take tiny stitches to look like holes in the 'cracker'

## Peanut People

**Unshelled peanuts** come in a wide variety of shapes, just like people Draw on faces with markers, then glue on bits of fabric to add clothes, hats, scarves, capes. Add yarn or embroidery thread hair. Bits of cotton balls make beards. glue a pin on the back

## Kites

Cut a diamond shape out of **craft foam.** Glue on **yarn** tail and a few tiny **bows** on tail

## Bedroll

Layer 2 different colored **felt** pieces, 2" X 4" rolled lengthwise, secure with two **yarn** ties.

## Snowman

Paint a **wooden ice cream spoon** white. Paint the top ½ inch black. Let dry. **Glue** on a scarf made of a scrap of **fabric,** draw on face and dots for buttons. Cut a circle of **black felt**, make slit to slide over top to form hat. Secure with glue.

## CD

Glue a paper label to a *poker chip*, with troop name, message or occasion

## Go Fish

Cut fish shape out of *fun foam.* Using a needle, run a *thread* from the mouth to a pole make of 3" *straw*. Tie knot at ends of thread

## Sundae

Glue *pompoms* into *clear plastic craft cups*. Add cut *coffee stir stick* for straw

## Frying Pan

*Paint* a *film canister lid* black. Glue a *bobby pin* to the bottom, extending to form a handle. Glue in 'bacon' and 'eggs' made of *white, orange, and brown felt*

## Pennants

Cut *craft foam* or felt triangle, add message, glue to short *dowel or toothpick*

## Real Book

Stack 3-4 rectangle *papers*, about 1" X 3". Sew down the center. Fold on stitching line to form book. Decorate cover, add title

## Flowerpot

Glue *tiny fabric or paper flowers* to the flat end of a *cork*

## Sit Upon

2" square **craft foam**, or felt, barely stuffed with pulled-apart **cotton ball**. Whip stitch edges.

## Peas in a Pod

Cut two 3" canoe shapes of **green felt**. Sew bottom edge of pod. Spread sides, and glue in 3-5 **green pompoms** to make peas

## Biffy Paper

*(*BIFFY stands for "bathroom in forest for you." Cute, but , oh, the *memories~!)*

The metal part of a clamp-type **clothes pin** is the holder. Glue a rolled strip of **white felt**, with end slightly trailing, for toilet paper

## Bat

Cut wing shapes out of **black craft foam**. Glue a **black pompom** to center, add **googly eyes**.

## Ants On A Log

Cut 1 ½ inch **twigs**, about 3/8 inch diameter. Glue on tiny **plastic ants** (found at party stores)

## Caterpillar

Coil length of **bumpy pipe cleaner** around **twig.** Glue on googly **eyes**

### Flip Flop Swap

Cut flip flop sole shapes from **craft foam**. Thread a needle with **thin ribbon,** and attach the strap part, knotting underneath

### Campfire
**Glue** small **twigs** into a log-cabin fire pattern. Add **felt or tissue paper** flame.

### Pompom Octopus

Braid 4 lengths of **yarn**, and glue the middle of the yarns on the bottom of pompom to make octopus arms.

### Pompom Spiders

Glue 4 long **black pipe cleaner** legs to the bottom of a **black pompom**. Bend pipe cleaner into spider's legs. Add **googly eyes** and a **string** to the top. Dry. Dangle, wait for screams.

### *BONUS SECTION: Recipes*

*This makes a smooth dough that resists cracking, even during intricate modeling, such as beads or features.*

## Bread Modeling Dough

2 slices day old white bread

2 tablespoons white glue

Cut crusts from bread. Break into small pieces in bowl. Mix in glue with your hands. Knead until it no longer sticks to your fingers, adding little bits of bread if needed to tame stickiness. Sculpt. Allow to dry 1-2 days. Paint with craft paints when dry

## Bubbles

1 cup **water**

5 Tablespoons **liquid dish detergent**

2 tablespoon **light corn syrup**.

Gently combine, taking care not to whip bubbles into it. Fashion a bubble wand out of pipe cleaners or wire

## Drink Mix Play Dough

*Makes vivid, scented dough (may color hands and surface--- I warned you!)*

Combine 1 cup **all-purpose flour**, 1 /2 cup **salt**. 3 T **cooking oil**, 1 package dry unsweetened drink mix (any flavor). Add in 1 cup **boiling water**, and stir to blend. Cool just enough to handle. Knead until smooth.

## One Day Play Dough

*This dough is very soft and easy to use, so break out the rolling pins and cookie cutters I find it much less messy if the artist has a clear boundary; usually "please keep it on the cookie sheet." It tends to be quite sticky when stored in a covered container, so we just make up a quick batch for One Day's play.*

Stir together 1 cup **all purpose flour** and 1 cup **salt.** Mix 1 cup **water** and few drops **food color** in a cup. Knead in only as much water as needed to make a soft smooth dough. Depending on air humidity, you may need more or less water or flour to make a smooth elastic dough.

## Awesome Sawdust Clay

*Sawdust is available for free at lumberyards, by the bucketful*

2/3 parts fine sawdust 1/ 3 part white flour

Mix in large bucket. Add **water,** stirring and kneading, just until it reaches stiff-but-squishy consistency. Get sculpting When dried in the sun, clay becomes very hard and can even be sanded.

## Sidewalk Chalk

Combine 1/3 cup **plaster of Paris** with 4 tablespoons **water**. Stir, then pour into **empty toilet tissue paper tubes** lined with waxed paper, or **empty juice boxes**. Allow to dry well. Peel off mold.

## Cornstarch OooGoo

*This is great fun  That rainy afternoon will pass before you know it. If some spills, let it dry; much easier to wipe up that way. It's a good idea to put down a plastic table cover first. You could add food color with the water, but it's plenty messy as it is. You may increase amounts; I've seen it mixed in full wading pools*

You'll need: cornstarch and water. That's it  The proportions are roughly half as much water as cornstarch.  To start, mix **one cup water** and **2 cups cornstarch** in a baking pan (9X13" is fine), adding the starch in small increments. You'll know you're doing it right when the mixture becomes hard to stir. Let the fun begin  Poke it with a finger, try to pick up a handful, set the spoon in the Ooo Goo and see how it feels when you remove it.  It's liquid, right? But can you break it?

**A SHAMELESS PLEA:**

I hope you have been inspired by the ideas in this book, and I hope you'll think of me as you teach a new generation how to expand their creative young minds.

I also hope you'll pay me back, by writing a quick review. It'll take you under three minutes, less time than it takes to break out craft supplies. You can even be anonymous. Five star reviews mean more than I can say, the literary equivalent of someone offering to entertain your chicken-pox-laden triplets on a rainy afternoon out of the blue. It's important to me and I appreciate it Happy Crafting

*Hungry Kids Campfire Cookbook*

Deb Graham

Copyright 2013

**Contents:**

Cooking Gear: ............................................................. 207
Feed Me Quick—It's Breakfast! ............................... 208
    Newspaper Eggs .................................................. 209
    Bacon and Eggs in a Paper Bag ......................... 210
    Breakfast Eggs in a Nest .................................... 210
    Omelet in a Bag ........................... with Hot Cocoa 211
    Homemade Hot Cocoa Mix ................................. 211
    Fried Eggs in Pepper Rings ............................... 212
    French Toast ........................................................ 213
    Stuffed French Toast ........................................... 213
    Apple Almost Pancakes ...................................... 214
Grub On The Go .......................................................... 217
    Trail GORP ........................................................... 217
    Tromping Trail Mix ............................................... 218
    Bird Seed Snack Mix ........................................... 218
    Ranch Snack Mix ................................................. 220
Mid Day Munchies and Snacks ................................. 220
    Sucking Orange ................................................... 221
    Tics on a Latrine Seat ......................................... 221
    Wormy Apples ..................................................... 221
    Ants on a Log ...................................................... 222
    Mosquitoes on a Stick ......................................... 222
    Walking Apples .................................................... 223
    Nutty Pretzel Wands ............................................ 223

Campfire Popcorn    (1 serving) ................................224
    Kettlecorn Variation...................................................224
    Edible Campfire ...........................................................224
Quick Lunches.........................................................................227
    Lunch in a Cone..........................................................227
    Boiled Quesadilla ........................................................227
    Tuna Melteds ...............................................................228
    Octopus Hot Dogs........................................................229
    Hot Dog Spiders (variation).........................................229
    Pita Pizza .....................................................................230
    Cheese Quesadilla......................................................231
    Really Fast Bean Burrito .............................................231
    Nachos..........................................................................231
    Lunch Munch Kabobs ..................................................232
    Drug Store Wrap ..........................................................235
    Flaming Hot Dog ..........................................................241
    Newspaper Whole Fish................................................241
    Grilled Pizza .................................................................242
Pioneer Drumsticks ................................................................243
(serves 6) ................................................................................243
    Sausage Pucks with Magic Sauce..............................244
    Magic Sauce ................................................................245
    Chicken Stir Fry ...........................................................245
    Saucy Barbecue Biscuits .............................................251
Go Withs and Side Dishes .....................................................253
    Corn On The Cob.........................................................253

    In The Coals Sweet Potatoes ................................... 253

    River Gelatin ............................................................. 254

    Super Refreshing Fruit Salad ................................... 254

    Grilled Pineapple ...................................................... 255

    Salad-on-a-Stick ...................................................... 256

    Asparagus Rafts ...................................................... 256

    Grilled Vegetables ................................................... 257

    Zucchini and Tomatoes in foil ................................. 257

    Fruit Skewers and Dip .............................................. 257

Warm and Comforting Breads ......................................... 259

    Orange Peel Muffins ................................................ 259

    Orange Peel Brownies ............................................. 260

    Pan Fried Biscuits .................................................... 260

    Oh, My Olive Bread .................................................. 260

    Almost Instant Rice Pudding .................................... 261

    Campfire Mini Pineapple Upside-down Cake .............. 262

    Fruit Pie .................................................................... 262

    Cinnamon Snakes on a Stick .................................. 263

    Campfire Peaches ................................................... 263

    Dirt in a Bag ............................................................. 264

    Snow Camping Ice Cream ....................................... 264

    Donuts ...................................................................... 265

    Campfire Éclairs ....................................................... 265

    Pudding Cones ........................................................ 266

    Cinnamon Snowflake Crisps .................................... 267

    Oh, No, It Melted Dessert Bars ................................ 267

- S'mores ... 267
- ...and Variations ... 268
- S'macos ... 268
- Plastic Bag Spoon Fudge ... 269
- Tiny Cookie Pizzas ... 270
- Cold Fried Eggs ... 270
- Very Nearly Thin Mints ... 271
- Fruit Pie ... 272
- Grilled Banana Boats ... 272
- Angels on Horseback ... 273
- Campfire Dessert Cones ... 273
- Campfire Baked Apples (version one) ... 274
- Campfire Baked Apples (version two) ... 274

a Plea: ... 275

## *Hungry Kids Campfire Cookbook*

Yay—a camping trip makes great memories! Many will center around food, as both familiar and novel meals are produced like magic, without even a kitchen stove Kids will be amazed at what they can make, and what adults pull together for them to enjoy. Simple foods can be good and fancy. There is no reason to sacrifice nutrition for good taste Sure, kids will enjoy hot dogs and marshmallows while camping, but how about some Chicken Stir Fry or Really Fast Bean Burritos, too?

The recipes in here *are* kid-friendly, but adults will find new favorites, too. Garlicky Shrimp with Asparagus Rafts and Fruit Kebabs are fancy enough to serve for company, not just as camp Enjoy reading through this book, as inspiration strikes you.

New cooking methods will make delicious memories, including breakfast in a zip-type bag, muffins in orange peels, fish in newspaper, and blueberry pie in foil. Did you notice that list included no pans to wash? This book includes simple recipes and some fancy ones, all designed for good nutrition and great memories.   Above all, make sure camp food is fun and plentiful---camping makes everybody hungry

Snacks for those on-the-go days are here, along with a good helping of desserts. Rice Pudding, Pineapple Upside Down Cake, Grilled Peaches... is your mouth watering yet?

I'm a mom, and a grandmother. I was a Girl Scout and leader for ten years, including four summers leading at a Girl Scout day camp. I also served a couple of three year stints as a Cub Scout den mother, and several years at Cub Scout Day Camp. On top of that, I live in the pacific Northwest, where rainy days –no, weeks -- are the norm. Our motto is "if we stay home until the weather is ideal, we may not get outdoors for month, so let's GO!"

Camping and nature requires energy and fuel for busy young –and old--bodies. I was on a week-long camping trip, obviously planned by someone else, who was on a weight-loss plan. Every breakfast was melon, *just melon,* and every single lunch and dinner was bagged green salad with low-fat dressing. That's it---no protein, no grains or carbs, no variety. There was widespread grumbling on Day One. By Day Two, hunger was an issue Day Three brought a mutiny, and a trip to town to buy real food. A campout is not the time to enforce weight loss You may avoid donuts at home, but at camp, they're fun!

Of course, enlisting the kids in the cooking process is great---it's part of the fun, and they feel like they're needed (which they are!), as well as making their appetites surge. Even timid eaters can't resist food *they* helped make

Cooking with children also teaches them life skills. I actually met a ten year old on a scout camping trip who didn't know how to cut a tomato...at home, her Mom did all the cooking. This girl was most enthusiastic, once I showed her how to hold a common kitchen knife. You'll enjoy seeing the pride in a camper's eyes when they announce "I helped make this!"

Kids are not the only ones making memories; the adults need time to play and explore, too This is not the time for three-hour meal prep. Really delicious food can be made in a short time, with a little planning.

You can cut down on prep time at camp by doing some of it at home. For example, you can cut meat at home, then freeze it *with its marinade ingredients* in a zip-type bag. Take it to camp like that; in the cooler, it'll help keep other foods cold, and as it thaws, it's ready to cook. You may want to do some slicing at home, if your stir-fry requires several vegetables. Having them at hand in a bag ready to toss in the pot makes for quick cooking at camp.

Don't turn up your nose at prepared or convenience foods in the grocery store as you plan your outing. Bags of frozen vegetable mixes are tasty (and fast), as are frozen hash browns. The produce aisle has bagged cole slaw that is nice in Oriental recipes, and a lot faster to use than whacking up cabbage, onions, carrots, and all. You can even buy pre-cut fruit and vegetables. Minute Rice makes a tasty brown rice that takes a short time to prepare, your local bulk food section has dehydrated vegetables and beans, and you might even pick up some dinner ideas while wandering the frozen food aisle. What's wrong with warming a thawed egg roll on a stick over a camp fire while the stir-fry cooks?

**The main thing is, make food fun, be creative, and get outdoors**

**Cooking Gear:**

*Camp food needs to be fun, not a chore. In my camping experience, I find I dislike doing clean up every bit as much as I do at home. My entire camping pot-and-pans stash consists of:*

**a large pot** for boiling water

a non-stick or well-seasoned **wok** for one-pot meals, steaming, and frying

a **flat griddle** for French toast and the like

**newspaper**

**bamboo skewers** for kebabs

**heavy duty aluminum foil**

quart sized **zip type freezer bags**

**a spatula** for turning

**cooking sticks** green sticks, often found at camp, debarked, about 28 " long and thumb diameter, OR uncoated metal coat hangers, straightened, OR store-bought cooking sticks, often sold with wooden handles. Some recipes require the fatter ones; most will use either type

*that's it*

Add in a few bowls, knives, and spoons, and a cutting board, and off I go

The **"pantry" part of the "kitchen"** has spices, herbs, and condiments, chosen just for that trip's menu. You don't need to pack your whole pantry -- premeasure spice mixes into little foil packets for each meal, labeled, of course. I figure out the foods I plan to cook, and bring those ingredients, , plus more snacks than I think we'll need, because camping makes the appetite soar. Our kids rave about the foods we made at camp, often bragging to friends whose entire menu consisted of hot dogs and canned beans.

You'll find amounts and servings to be very flexible in this book. Adapt, change it up, have fun

## Feed Me Quick—It's Breakfast!

*The quickest way to stop campers from grumbling "I'm hungry!" is to give them a job to help make their own breakfast. These first recipes are each-one-make-one.*

### Newspaper Eggs
*Egg will be clean and taste like a boiled egg, with no pot to wash*

Wrap raw eggs in newspaper, one per full sheet. Soak newspaper in water. Bury in hot coals. Dig out after 5-8 minutes (depending on desired doneness). Peel off paper and egg shell.

## Bacon and Eggs in a Paper Bag

*Dramatic breakfast, with no cleanup Eat it right from the bag. Choose a sturdy cooking stick to hold the bag.*

Open a brown paper lunch sack, and line the bottom with sliced bacon, cut to fit, one layer deep. Crack 2 eggs onto bacon Sprinkle eggs with salt and pepper. . Roll the top of the bag halfway down, like a cuff, leaving the top open. Poke a cooking stick through bag, under the rolls. Using the stick as handle, hold the bag 4-5 inches over the fire or coals until eggs are cooked, about 8-10 minutes.

## Breakfast Eggs in a Nest

*Even better with grated cheese on top*

Cut a hole in a slice of buttered bread. Save the cut out part. Lay bread on griddle or skillet. Crack one egg into center of hole. Cook until set, then turn over and finish cooking egg. Toast the cut out part in pan as egg cooks. Salt and pepper to taste.

## Omelet in a Bag     ....with Hot Cocoa

*Make up the Mix at home, then use hot water from your **Omelets in a Bag** to make hot cocoa at camp.*
*Not like you cook at home No pan to scrub, and even the youngest campers can put their own bag together, with little help.*

Bring a pot of water to a stiff simmer, at least 4 inches deep. In a zip-type freezer bag, combine 2 eggs, and a few spoons of omelet ingredients as desired (chopped onion, bell pepper, diced ham, bacon bits, leftover vegetables from dinner, spinach, shredded cheese, whatever sounds good). Sprinkle in salt and pepper.

Seal the bag, squeezing out as much air as possible. Squish to combine. Suspend in water, using a clothes pin to secure to the edge of the pot. Simmer about 8 minutes, pinching with potholder-covered hand once during cooking. Eat right from the bag.

HINT: The omelet must cook about 3 minutes past when it looks done, otherwise the eggs will be runny in the center.

## Homemade Hot Cocoa Mix

*Ideal use for those leftover candy canes!*

2 cups nonfat dry milk
1 cup white sugar
1/2 cup cocoa
1/2 cup non-dairy creamer
miniature marshmallows
crushed peppermint candies (optional)

Combine ingredients and mix well. Store in an airtight container or zip-type bag. Add 4 tablespoons of mix to a mug and add very hot water. Stir.

## Fried Eggs in Pepper Rings

*Try different colors of peppers for a pretty presentation. Save the non-ring parts of the peppers for another recipe*

Grease a skillet or griddle. Slice a bell pepper crosswise into rings, about 3/4 inch thick, removing seeds. Place each slice on the griddle, and cook for one minute. Carefully break one egg into each pepper ring. Cook until set, then flip, or leave sunny-side-up. Sprinkle with salt and pepper.

## French Toast

*French Toast is easy at camp, and it's more nutritious than plain old pancakes. It's easy to multiply, and a good way to use up leftover bread, rolls, or hot dog buns.*

For each serving: Beat 1 egg with 3 T milk. Soak 2 slices of bread (or 2 hamburger buns, English muffins, what have you) in the egg mixture while the pan heats. Melt 1 t butter in pan (or use cooking spray). Slide bread into pan. Cook until golden, flip, and cook other side until golden. Serve with jam, syrup, or cut up fruit.

## Stuffed French Toast

*Strawberry jam is especially delicious You won't need syrup.*

Make same as French Toast, except: before dipping in the egg and milk mixture, make a sandwich by spreading cream cheese and jam inside the bread, or buns.

## Breakfast Burritos     (serves 4)

*Frozen hash browns make this easy*

  Brown 1 lb breakfast sausage in skillet. Drain all but 1 T fat.  Add 4 cups frozen hash browns  or diced potatoes. Cook, stirring,  until potatoes are soft (they may not brown) . Lightly beat 8 eggs, and add to pan, stirring frequently, until mostly set.  Divide mixture onto 8 flour tortillas, sprinkle with grated cheddar cheese, and wrap, folding in sides as you go.

## Apple Almost Pancakes

*Breakfast with a hole in the middle*

Mix add-water-only pancake batter as directed on the package. Dip cored apple rings into batter, and fry on a greased griddle, as if you're making pancakes. Turn to brown both sides. Serve with cinnamon/sugar or syrup.

## Breakfast Oblets (serves 5)

*This dish was named by a cute 5 year old, who couldn't pronounce "omelet." It's also good with frozen hash browns*

Brown 1 lb bulk sausage in a frying pan. Add 4-5 cups potatoes, diced. Cook until potatoes are tender. Drain grease. Sprinkle with 1 cup chopped vegetables (bell peppers, spinach, broccoli, etc). Lightly beat 8 eggs with 1 T water, and pour over the pan. Sprinkle with salt and pepper. As eggs cook, gently lift edges to allow raw eggs to reach bottom of the pan. Serve when eggs are nearly set. Cut into wedges.

## Best Ever Breakfast Glop (serves 4)

*Really, have you ever had bad Glop? Leftover baked potatoes from dinner? Great None? Cook potatoes in butter until soft first, then continue. It helps to have two people; one to cook Glop, one to make Glop Sauce*

**Glop:** Melt 3 tablespoons butter in a large skillet. Toss in 3 cooked, sliced potatoes, 1 cup ham cubes, salt and pepper, and cook 4 minutes. Meanwhile, make **Glop Sauce,** below. Stir together five lightly beaten eggs and 1 /2 cup diced bell pepper. Stir until eggs are nearly done, and top with Glop Sauce and 1/2 cup grated cheddar cheese

***Glop Sauce**:* Melt 3 T butter in a pan, with 3 T flour and a sprinkle of salt and pepper. Add in 1 1/ 4 cup milk while stirring. Bring to a boil, stirring frequently. Set aside and finish Glop.

*Variations: stir in cooked fish, spinach, other cheeses, cooked bacon or sausage...be creative*

## Breakfast Pizza   (2 servings)

Melt 1 T butter in a pan. Lightly cook 1/2 bell pepper (diced) with 4 eggs, stirring to scramble. Split 2 English muffins, and spread 1 T bottled spaghetti sauce on each. Top with 4 slices pepperoni, grated mozzarella cheese, and evenly divide the eggs for each pizza. Return to pan, cover with foil, and warm until cheese melts slightly.

## Grub On The Go

*Here are snack ideas for hikers or campers too busy to sit and eat Sizes are very flexible, depending on group's size. Make ahead and store in individual zip-type bags or larger air-tight container.*

### Trail GORP

*Did you know that GORP stands for "Good Old Raisins and Peanuts"?*

The traditional mix is always M&M's, raisins and peanuts. Try including tiny ranch flavored crackers, fish crackers, small pretzels, dried fruit, salted nuts, banana chips, freeze-dried pineapple bits, dried apples, coconut, sunflower seeds, unsweetened dry cereal, shoestring potatoes, small candies, chocolate chips, pretzels, peanut butter chips, etc.

## Tromping Trail Mix

Melt 1 tbs. butter in a pan. Stir in 1 cup peanuts, and 1/4 cup sunflower seeds. Stir as they brown, 2-4 minutes. Remove from heat, and add in 1 1/4 cup raisins, and 12-15 dried apricots, cut in thin slices. Cool before packaging.

## Bird Seed Snack Mix

*Lightweight lunch, to nibble slowly on a hike, or eat it as a snack at a rest stop.*

Combine equal amounts of: sugar coated cereal, candy coasted chocolates, roasted nuts, raisins, and chow mien noodles

## Famous Puppy Chow

*Nobody knows why this is famous. It just ...is.*

Melt 1/4 cup butter, 1 cup chocolate chips, and 3/4 cup peanut butter. Pour over
8 cups woven squares cereal (like rice chex) and stir well. Put 2 cups powdered sugar in a large paper bag. Add cereal mixture and shake well to coat evenly.

### Sunshine Munchies

Combine equal amounts shelled sunflower seeds, pumpkin seeds, raisins, peanuts or cashews or other nuts, and dried cranberries

### Seashore Snack Mix

*Perfect for beach camping*

Combine equal amounts: dry chow mein noodles (seaweed), pretzel sticks (driftwood), fish crackers (fish), dried pineapple (sea glass), golden raisins (fish eggs), roasted peanuts (beach pebbles), ring-shaped cereal (life preservers)

### Go Go Gobbledy-Gook

*Stir together:*

 4 cups dry rice cereal
1 cup chopped peanuts
1 cup raisins, chopped dates, chopped prunes, or diced apricots
1 cup sunflower seeds
1 cup pretzel sticks

## Ranch Snack Mix

*who doesn't love ranch flavor?*

8 cups woven squares cereal (like chex)
2 1/2 cups pretzel sticks or twists
2 1/2 cups bite size cheddar cheese crackers
3 tablespoons cooking oil
1-1 oz package powdered Ranch salad dressing mix

Mix cereal, pretzels, and crackers. Pour oil over cereal mixture. Close bag and toss mix until well coated with oil. Add ranch dressing mix and close bag. Toss mix until well coated.

## Mid Day Munchies and Snacks

*Three meals a day just won't cut it when campers are on the go This section has snack recipes for mid-day energy boosts, with minimal prep.*

## Sucking Orange

*Pass the wipes*

Roll an orange around in your hand to smoosh the insides up, taking care not to rip the peel. Make a tiny X with a knife near the stem end of the orange. Insert a peppermint stick (the old fashioned kind that are semi-porous and have a slight hole in the middle; experiment with some and you'll find the right ones) into the orange. Sip the orange juice through the peppermint "straw." Squeeze the orange as you sip. When it runs dry, tear apart the orange and eat it.

## Tics on a Latrine Seat

Spread cream cheese on a cored apple ring, and add raisins in a ring on top

## Wormy Apples

*Eeeww...the kids will love these* Spread apple wedges with peanut butter. Wrap 2-3 gummi worms around each.

## Ants on a Log

Cut 3-4" celery sticks, and fill with peanut butter. Top with raisins in a row.

## Mosquitoes on a Stick

*Similar to Ants on a Log, but of course, mosquitoes are smaller.*

Cut 3-4" celery sticks, and fill with peanut butter. Top with sunflower seeds

## Antelope Lips (serves 2)

Cut red apple into eight wedges, top to bottom, and trim away seeds. Spread one side of each with peanut butter or caramel dip. Sandwich 4-5 mini marshmallows between 2 apple wedges for antelope teeth

## Walking Apples

*Quick energy for a hike*

Hollow out one apple per person, leaving the bottom intact, with 1" walls. Chop up the apple bits (minus seeds). Stir in a handful of raisins and just enough peanut butter to hold filling together. Pack the filling into the apple shell, and eat while walking or hiking.

## Nutty Pretzel Wands

*Peanut allergies? Substitute crunchy dry cereal or sunflower seeds for peanuts, and almond butter for peanut butter. Also tasty with chocolate frosting.*

Spread peanut butter on the top few inches of a long pretzel rod. Roll in chopped peanuts.

## Campfire Popcorn    (1 serving)

*Hot, crunchy, noisy foods---what can be better? Even better drizzled with butter, salt, parmesan cheese, bacon bits...be creative!*

Place 2 tablespoons popcorn kernels and 2 tablespoons cooking oil in the center of a large square of heavy-duty aluminum foil. Fold the edges to form a loose pouch, leaving plenty of room for the kernels to pop. Tie a corner of the pouch to a cooking stick with a piece of string. Shake over a fire or coals until popping almost stops.

## **Kettlecorn** Variation

Same as Campfire Popcorn, except add 1 T sugar and 1/2 tsp salt before folding foil.

## Edible Campfire

*This is a fun way to teach fire building technique. Let children arrange each ingredient on a plate in order listed, explaining fire safety and fire building as you go.*

*Rice cake* spread with *peanut butter or cream cheese* (fire pit)

*Large bread stick* or pretzel sticks (fuel)

*shoestring potatoes* or *small pretzel sticks* (kindling)

*Shredded cheese*, or *coconut* ( tinder)

*mini marshmallows, raisins, or tiny gumdrops* (stones for fire circle)

*Candy corn or red hot candy* (to light fire)

Small *lollipop* (shovel)

Cup of *water* (water bucket)

Lollipop (shovel)

shoestring potatoes (fuel)
large pretzels (logs)
cheese coconut or (tinder)
candy corn (fire)
cookie (fire pit)
mini marshmallows (fire ring)

drink (water bucket)

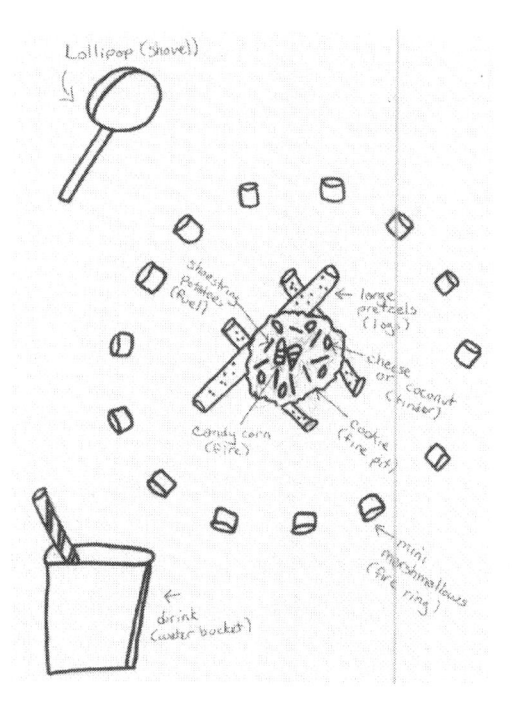

## Quick Lunches

*Again, few amounts are given, because these recipes are flexible, depending on size of the group*

### Lunch in a Cone

**Plain ice cream cones** make great non-messy portable "dishes" for chicken salad, tuna salad, cole slaw, etc –and no clean up Don't make them too far ahead, though, as they will get soggy.

### Boiled Quesadilla

*Tip: Securing with a spring-type clothespin to side of pot makes this easy to retrieve.*

Bring a pot of water to a boil. Sprinkle shredded jack or cheddar cheese and chopped green onions on a flour tortilla. Fold so all filling is inside, tucking in sides, like an eggroll. Place in zip-type freezer bag, and seal so most of the air is squished out. Place in gently boiling water until warm and melty.

## Tuna Melteds

*A warm, melty sandwich can't be beat!*

Prepare a simple tuna salad using drained tuna, mayonnaise, pickle relish, and grated cheddar cheese. Spread inside buns, any shape. Wrap in foil and cook on griddle or over coals until name is obvious.

**Variation:** use cooked chicken, or fish, instead of tuna.

## Traditional Hot Dogs in a Blanket

*Sometimes the old stand bys are new to youngsters. Besides, they stood the test of time because they're <u>good</u>*

Wrap each hot dog in a refrigerated crescent roll sheet, sealing the ends of the dough, leaving hot dog ends exposed. Slip the hot dog onto a cooking stick, length wise. Cook slowly over the coals until the roll is golden brown, turning frequently. Dip in ketchup

## Octopus Hot Dogs

Carefully slice a hot dog lengthwise, leaving 1" at one end uncut for the" head," and cut into long "legs." Eight "legs" is ideal, six is easier Drop in boiling water, and cook until "legs" curl up. Serve open face on sliced bread with condiments.

### Hot Dog Spiders (variation)

*Do kids get to eat spiders at home?*

Carefully cut 4 slits lengthwise on hot dog, from each end, leaving 1" middle intact for "body." Cook in water, or impale center on stick over coals. It's done when the "legs" curl up.

### Hot Dog People (variation)

Decide which end is the "head." Cut lengthwise 2-3 inches from the other end, leaving the "legs" attached. Cut a slit on each "shoulder" down the side of the hot dog for "arms." As they cook, body parts will curl and look like...well, people. Dots of mustard make great eyes.

## Walking Tacos ( serves 8)

*Eat out of the bag –no plates to wash!*

Brown 1 lb ground beef in a pan. Add taco seasoning packet and water as directed on package. Simmer until nearly dry.

To serve, slit open top of 8 individual bags of corn chips. Sprinkle in taco meat, and top with 12 oz grated cheddar cheese. May also add shredded lettuce, black olives, and diced tomatoes, canned beans (drained), salsa, sour cream---it's *your* lunch

## Pita Pizza

*These are brag-worthy, and simple to make*

Slice a flap in pita bread, at the edge, about 3 /4 around bread. Spread pizza sauce or jarred pasta sauce inside, add grated mozzarella or jack cheese, pepperoni, vegetables, and other pizza toppings as desired. Replace flap. Wrap in foil. Heat on coals or grill until hot, turning once or twice.

## Cheese Quesadilla

*Quick lunch, side, or snack. Leftover meat from last night's dinner goes well here*

Sprinkle grated cheddar or jack cheese and black olives on a flour tortilla. Heat in flat pan or grill over medium heat until cheese is melted. Fold in half. Dip in salsa

## Really Fast Bean Burrito

*Check your local natural foods store or bulk foods section for dehydrated refried beans. In a pinch, canned beans are okay.*

Rehydrate beans in a zip-type bag, according to directions. Cut corner off bag, and squeeze some beans onto a flour tortilla. Add grated cheddar cheese and salsa and you have a fast crowd -pleasing lunch entree.

## Nachos

*Be as creative as you'd like, by adding other ingredients, such as leftover taco meat, shredded chicken or beef, chopped vegetables, avocado, canned black beans (drained), jalapenos, diced tomatoes, whatever sounds good*

Arrange corn chips in a disposable aluminum pie pan. Top with shredded cheddar or jack cheese. Add in other ingredients as desired. Wrap in foil, covering pan completely and leaving a fold at the top to make a handle. Poke a cooking stick or tongs through the handle, and hold over coals to warm through. Or, set directly on grill. When cheese is melted, open, and top with salsa.

## Lunch Munch Kabobs

*A nice change of pace from plain old hot dogs*

Soak bamboo skewers in water at least 30 minutes. Cut hot dogs or Polish sausages into 1" chunks. String on skewers with canned or fresh pineapple chunks. Grill until hot through. Serve in hot dog buns

*Variation: substitute ham cubes for hot dogs. Add mushrooms or zucchini chunks instead of pineapple.*

## Look, Ma, No Pans (Foods in Foil)

### Foil dinners

*are easy to make, with endless variety They're best in one-person servings, but make as many packets as you want. The nice thing about this is that each person can customize it to their taste, adding extra peas, or leaving out the yucky carrots.*

*You can use beef, pork, chicken, lamb, goat, yak, seafood, just about any vegetable you like... even frozen vegetables. Be aware of food sizes, so the meal will cook evenly. Simply layer any raw meat or seafood, pounded thin or cut in bite-sized chunks, plus sliced onions, potatoes, carrots, and other vegetables as desired onto a large sheet of heavy duty foil. Add seasonings, herbs, mushroom soup, soy sauce, teriyaki, barbecue sauce, etc. Steam does the cooking; if your ingredients seem dry, add a little liquid (juice, an ice cube, water, broth, and so on).*

*Fold in drugstore wrap fashion, taking care to enclose everything tightly. Cook on coals or hot grill, turning 2-3 times during cooking period. Always use a brand-name heavy-duty foil...I find some of the store brands are wimpier than the regular foil If I don't have heavy-duty foil, I use two layers of regular foil.*

***A foolproof trick:*** *Assemble your dinner, fold foil closed, then wrap the entire foil package in very wet newspaper, 2-3 sheets thick. Wrap in another layer of foil, being as neat as possible, and taking care to seal edges well. Dinner will be perfectly done ---and not burnt!-- when newspaper layer is dry.*

***Another tip,*** *especially if you disregard the wet newspaper tip: layer your meal with vegetables that can tolerate potential scorching on the top and bottom of the package. For example, toasted onions are fine, but burnt potatoes are yucky.*

### Drug Store Wrap

***Drugstore wrap*** *is the best way to fold foil dinners.*

*It holds in all the juices and flavor.*

*Start with a large sheet of heavy duty foil. Place food in the center of the foil.*

Fold top down, twice. then fold in ends, twice, pressing to seal packet.

## Sausage Cabbage Stew in foil (serves 4)

*The cheese makes a warm sauce*

Lay out 4 large sheets heavy-duty foil. Divided evenly on each packet:

1 small head cabbage, cut in 1" pieces

1 pound smoked or Polish sausage, cut in 1/4" slices

1 large onion, diced

1 bell pepper, diced

4 medium potatoes, cut in 1" pieces

2 large carrots, cut in 1/4" slices

4 T butter

4 slices American cheese

salt and pepper to taste

Fold foil to seal each meal. Place on rack over medium heat for one hour, turning a few times, or until tender.

### Jerk Chicken Wings (1 serving)

Toss 6 split chicken wings, 2 t vegetable oil and 3 tablespoons jerk seasoning on a sheet of foil. Form a foil packet. Grill over high heat, turning once, about 25 minutes. Even better with lime juice sprinkled on top.

### Italian Meatballs in foil  (serves 4)

*Wet hands make it easier to shape meatballs. Even better served with crusty bread.*

Mix 3 slices bread, torn up, with 1 pound bulk Italian sausage. Shape into 20 meatballs. Set aside.

Chop one small onion and 4 cups of cabbage. Divide onto 4 sheets of heavy duty foil. Sprinkle each with salt and pepper, and 1/2 tsp garlic powder. Arrange meatballs on top. Pour 1/3 cup tomato sauce or bottled pasta sauce on meatballs. Fold foil into packets, sealing edges tightly. Cook on medium coals or grate, turning every so often.

## Foiled Fish And Veggies (each packet serves 2-3)

*In a classy restaurant, this would be an elegant meal served in parchment paper. Camping, it's a yummy foil dinner, with no clean up The salad dressing steams the vegetables, while making a wonderful sauce.*

1 lb fresh fish, whole or fillets, cleaned

1 small onion, sliced thin

2 potatoes, sliced

2 carrots, sliced

zucchini or other summer squash, sliced

1 lemon, sliced thin (optional)

bottled Italian salad dressing

Wrap fish and vegetables in heavy duty foil wrap, leaving one end open. Pour in a liberal amount of salad dressing. Close the foil tightly so as to keep steam in during cooking. Place on medium heat grill or near coals of campfire. Cook gently until potatoes and carrots are cooked through.

## Garlicky Shrimp in foil

Mix 1/2 stick softened butter, 1 cup chopped parsley, 2 minced garlic cloves, and salt and pepper. Toss with the juice of 1 lemon, 1 pound unpeeled large shrimp and a pinch of red pepper flakes. Divide between 2 foil packets. Grill over high heat, 8 minutes.

## Stuffed Peppers (serves 4)

*Pretty meal with yellow, red, or orange peppers, but green is just fine. Spoon additional sauce over peppers when done, if you'd like.*

Cut tops off 4 bell peppers and set aside. Take out veins and seeds. Mix 1 lb ground beef or chicken, 1/2 cup water, 1 1/ 3 cups dry Minute Rice, 1 /2 cup chopped onion, 1 tsp garlic powder, 1 /4 tsp each salt and pepper, 1/4 cup grated parmesan cheese, and 1/2 cup tomato sauce, pizza sauce, or ketchup. Stuff peppers with meat mixture. Put tops back on, and wrap each tightly in foil. Cook over coals about 20 minutes, until cooked through. As they are nearly done, your hint is that they begin to they smell wonderful

**Variation:** *use bulk Italian sausage instead of beef. It's also great with summer squash instead of bell peppers. Just slice in half and scoop out seeds to make canoe shapes.*

## Yum, It's Supper Time!

(main dishes )

*Supper's the time to go all out. Activities are winding down, appetites are gearing up, and it's time for some memorable food*

## Flaming Hot Dog

*A dramatic meal with no clean up You don't even need a campfire. This is perfect for the last day of camping. Serves one, but you can easily arrange a circle of flaming hot dogs for a group.*

Wash and dry an empty <u>paper</u> milk carton, one quart or half gallon size.   Place a hot dog in a bun. Wrap in foil. Put the wrapped hot dog in the carton, standing up. Set it in a fire pit, and light the top of the milk carton in a few places. By the time the carton is burnt to the ground, the hot dog will be perfectly cooked, inside a toasted bun

## Newspaper Whole Fish

*This is a delicious way to cook that fresh fish you just caught Suggested seasonings: lemon juice, lemon slices, orange slices, onion slices, dill, diced bell pepper, salt and pepper, seasoning salt mix, lemon pepper. If you prefer not to have the fish touch the newspaper directly, wrap it first in a layer of brown kraft paper.*

Clean and scale the fish. Brush outside with oil, and season inside. Roll tightly in several sheets of newspaper, folding ends in to make a tidy package. Dunk fish and newspaper in water to saturate. Place fish directly on hot coals or a hot grill. Cook approximately 10 minutes per side. If newspaper dries out before fish is done, remove from heat and spray with water, or add another layer of wet paper, then return to fire. Cooking time will vary depending on size of fish and heat source. Unwrap to eat. Often skin will stick to the paper, making serving even easier.

## Grilled Pizza
(6 single serving pizzas)

*It sounds like it won't turn out, but it does, and it's wonderful You have to assemble it fast, so have the toppings ready to go before you cook the dough*

*Even easier: combine crust ingredients, except water, in a zip-type bag at home, then mix at camp.*

*A hot tent on a sunny afternoon is ideal place to raise the dough*

CRUST:

4 cups flour (bread flour for crispy crust, all purpose for chewy crust), 1 t sugar, 2 t or one envelope dry yeast, 2 t salt. At camp, mix in 1 1 /2 cups warm water. Knead lightly 5 minutes. Place in warm spot to rise for one hour.

Divide dough into 6 pieces. Stretch dough to make individual pizzas, about 6" each. Brush lightly with oil, or spritz with cooking spray. Place directly on grill. Grill over medium heat until bottom has marks, about 2-3 minutes. Turn, and cook another minute. Working quickly, spread prepared pizza or pasta sauce on crusts. Add mozzarella cheese, and whatever other toppings you desire. Tent loosely with foil and grill another minute or two until cheese starts to melt.

*Topping ideas:* pepperoni, cooked sausage, herbs, onions, bell peppers, sliced olives, seafood, ham bits, cooked chicken, bacon, pineapple, anchovies, mushrooms, artichokes, parmesan....endless combinations

## Pioneer Drumsticks

### (serves 6)

3 lb. ground beef, pork, bulk sausage, or chicken
1 cup corn flakes, crushed
2 eggs
salt, pepper, garlic powder to taste
medium onion, minced


12 wooden craft sticks, soaked in water

Mix ingredients thoroughly and divide into 12 portions. Wrap around the end of the sticks making the roll long and thin, leaving a couple of inches of stick exposed for a handle. Cook over coals, turning frequently, until cooked through. Eat off the stick, like a drumstick.

## Sausage Pucks with Magic Sauce

*The dough will seem crumbly, but work it in your hands and it will come together. Add a tsp of water at a time if you get desperate. The Magic Sauce is also delicious on lunchmeat or veggie sandwiches, and hot dogs.*

Combine: 1 pound raw bulk sausage (Italian, sweet, breakfast style or hot) with 4 cups grated sharp cheddar cheese and 3 cups baking mix (such as Bisquick). Work with your hands until it comes together. Shape into balls about Ping-Pong ball size, and flatten to 1 inch thickness. Cook in dry frying pan over medium heat until golden, turning once. Dip in Magic Sauce.

## Magic Sauce

*This tastes very complex, but couldn't be easier It's also great on cold sandwiches*

Stir together 1 cup mayonnaise with 1 1/ 2 tablespoons yellow mustard. You're done!

## Chicken Stir Fry

*Filling, nutritious meal, with endless variations. The sauce mixture can be made at home, and kept in cooler. Serve over cooked rice or pasta*

In a large covered pan, or wok, heat 3 T oil. Dust 2 lbs chicken strips with flour and brown in the oil. Set aside. In the same pan, cook 3 bags frozen Chinese-style vegetables, or 7 cups sliced assorted vegetables of your choice (broccoli, cabbage, squash, zucchini, onions, celery, pineapple chunks, water chestnuts) until crisp-tender. Combine 3 /4 cup soy sauce, 1 T ground ginger, 1 /2 cup brown sugar, 3 /4 cup water, 1 tsp pepper, and 1/3 cup cornstarch. Add to the pan, stirring and boiling for one minute. Put chicken back in the pan. Stir. Serve over cooked rice or pasta.

## Fresh Fish Chowder  (serves 6)

*A one-pot meal that's brag-worthy Serve with crusty bread or biscuits.*

Cook 2 slices bacon, diced, in a pot. Set aside. Add 1 sliced onion and 3 potatoes, (diced) to the bacon fat and cook until slightly browned. Stir in 2 T flour. Add 1 quart water and simmer 10 minutes, until potatoes are nearly tender. Cut 6 fish fillets into 1 inch cubes. Add fish, and simmer 5 minutes. Stir in 1 can evaporated milk, salt and pepper to taste, and 1 T butter. Simmer 5 minutes, stirring often so the milk will not burn.

## Taco Potatoes (serves 6)

*A full meal, in a potato You can make it fancier by substituting  mixed salad greens for lettuce*

Cut six baking potatoes in half. Drizzle with a little cooking oil, wrap in foil, and set on coals or grate to cook, turning occasionally. While potatoes cook, brown 1 lb ground beef. Drain off grease, and add one packet of taco seasoning mix, and water, and cook according to package directions. Chop 1/ 2 head lettuce. Grate 6 oz cheddar cheese.  Dice 2 tomatoes. When potatoes are soft, top each half with meat mixture, lettuce, tomatoes, 2 T sour cream, and bottled salsa.

## Burger Logs (serves 4)

*They're not pretty, but <u>are they good~</u> If you make them at home, freeze them, and cook from frozen state.*

Season 1 lb ground beef with dry onion soup mix. Form into 4 hot-dog shaped logs. Wrap each log with a slice of bacon, at an angle to cover most of meat. Secure with toothpick, if needed. Grill over medium heat, turning a few times, until cooked through. Serve in a hot dog bun with ketchup and mustard.

## Saucy Barbecue Biscuits

Fast, and delicious

Cook strips of chicken or beef in 2 T oil until nearly done. Pour bottled barbecue sauce over meat, and heat through. Serve over bread, toast, or biscuits.

## So Good Chicken Stew (serves 6-8)

*Delicious with biscuits or bread*

8-10 chicken thighs or breasts
1 cup flour
1 Tbs. poultry seasoning
salt and pepper
4 potatoes
4 large carrots
1 onion
bag frozen peas, or green beans, OR corn on the cob in 2" pieces

Cut potatoes, carrots, and onion into 1/2 inch chunks. Mix flour and seasonings in a plastic bag. Shake chicken pieces, one at a time, to coat. Repeat with potatoes. Heat large pot with ½ inch oil in it. Brown chicken, turning, till all sides are golden. Drain oil from pot. Add one inch of water. Place potatoes, carrots, and onions over chicken. Cook about 45 minutes until chicken is tender. Check every so often to ensure there is a small amount of water in the pot, adding a bit more if needed. Add in fresh peas, green beans, or corn on the cob, cut into 2 " chunks, the last five minutes of cooking time.

## Camp Sukiyaki  (serves 4)

*Fancy-smancy, at camp*

1 lb chicken, boned, cut into small strips

2 beef bouillon cubes

2 T sugar

1 cup water

1/3 cup soy sauce

5 cups vegetables (total), cut matchstick size (onion, celery, carrot, snow peas, bamboo shoots, water chestnuts, broccoli, etc)

2 cups fresh spinach, shredded coarsely

3 cups hot cooked rice (instant rice is easy while camping!)

Combine chicken, bullion, sugar, soy sauce and water in large wok or Dutch oven.  Simmer five minutes. Add in vegetables (not spinach), and cook until crisp-tender.  To serve, layer rice, raw spinach, and meat-vegetable-sauce mixture in bowls.

## Sticky Chicken (serves 4)

*Easy make-ahead meal that everyone will love! Parboiled rice is perfect here*

2 boneless skinless chicken breasts, cut into strips.

1/4 cup peanut butter

1 tablespoon honey

2 tablespoons soy sauce

1/4 teaspoon garlic powder

1/4 teaspoon cayenne pepper

1 tablespoon ketchup

salt and pepper, to taste

Combine the meat and marinade at home, then freeze in a large zip-type bag. Store in a cooler at camp. When you're ready to cook, break up chicken chunks. Cook over a medium heat in a large frying pan about 20 minutes, stirring often, until chicken is cooked through. Add 2-3 T of water if it seems too dry while cooking. Serve over rice or noodles.

## Super Quick Chicken Stir Fry (serves 4-6)

*Make the sauce at home, and keep cold in a zip-type bag. Make Minute Rice while the pan heats.*

**Sauce:** Combine in a zip-type bag: 1/4 cup soy sauce, 1 cup water, 1/2 teaspoon ground ginger, 1/2 teaspoon garlic powder, 5 tablespoons packed brown sugar, 2 tablespoons cornstarch.

In a wok or large pan, cook 1-2 lbs chicken cubes or strips in 2 T oil, until almost done through. Add in 2 bags any style frozen Chinese vegetables. Cook 4 minutes. Mix Sauce with 1 1/4 cup cold water, stirring to dissolve corn starch. Cook, stirring, until sauce is glossy and thickened, about 2 minutes. Sprinkle with 1 /2 cup cashews or peanuts. Serve over Minute Rice.

## Peppery Pepper Steak  (serves 4)

*Marinate the meat in a zip type bag for at least an hour. You can also mix the marinade at home, and freeze the beef in it. As it thaws, the flavor sinks into the meat. You'll want to soak up the tasty juices, so serve it over rice.*

1 lb tender beef steak, cut against the grain into strips, in a zip type bag with 1 cup soy sauce, 3 T sugar, 2 T vegetable oil, 1 T black pepper, 3 green onions, finely chopped, and 2 cloves minced garlic. Let stand, chilled, at least an hour. Cut 2 bell peppers, any color, into thin strips. Drain the meat and reserve the marinade. Cook the meat in a wok or large pan until just starting to brown. Add in the peppers, and cook 2 minutes. Add 3 T corn starch to the reserved marinade mixture. Push meat and peppers to sides of the pan, and cook sauce in the middle, stirring, until it turns glossy, about 3 minutes. Serve over rice or Minute Rice.

## Go Withs and Side Dishes

*I usually make part of a meal simple, such as watermelon or peaches from that nearby farm stand, as a side dish to a 'fancy' main dish.*

## Corn On The Cob

*Soaking the husks prevents kernels from burning, and steams the corn.*

Pull back husks on ears of corn, but don't remove husks. Pull off as much "hair" as you can. Fold husks back over corn. Soak ears in water for a few minutes. Cook on coals or grate, turning, for about 8-12 minutes. Pull back husks to serve. Sprinkle with butter, salt and pepper, chili powder, parmesan cheese, lime juice, or eat plain. Yum, any way you eat it

## In The Coals Sweet Potatoes

*Sweet and creamy sweet potatoes are more nutritious than white potatoes, and really delicious  Leftovers are good in salads or omelets.*

Wrap sweet potatoes in foil, and bury in hot coals until soft when squeezed with a potholder-covered hand. Turn them every so often as they roast. That's the whole recipe Because they are dense, sweet potatoes can take 45 minute to an hour to cook. They're great with butter and brown sugar, or salt and pepper.

## River Gelatin

*avoid citrus and pineapple---it prevents setting*

Mix any flavor powdered gelatin  and very warm water in a zip-type plastic bag, following package directions for amount. Squish and shake to dissolve gelatin.  Add slightly less cold water than on instructions. Add cut up fruit if desired. Seal bag, squeezing out a much air as possible. Place into another bag, removing air, then secure with a rock in a flowing river to weight it down. Retrieve when gelatin is gelled.

## Super Refreshing Fruit Salad

*This is an easy everyone-contribute-something treat for a large group; have each person bring a different fruit, cut into bite size pieces, then combine together. Stone fruit, berries, melons, kiwi, pineapple, apples, pears, grapes, and citrus are all delicious.*

Combine any combination of cold, cut up fresh fruit in a large bowl or bucket. Pour cold ginger ale over the fruit, about 2 inches deeper than the fruit. Scoop up fruit and soda into cups for a refreshing treat after a hike on a hot day.

## Grilled Pineapple

*Is this a side dish, or dessert? Either way, it'll be a favorite*

Cut away the outer parts of a whole pineapple, and slice horizontally into one inch thick slices. Rub both sides with brown sugar, and grill until golden, turning once.

Variation: cut long spears instead of slices.

## Salad-on-a-Stick

*Why does everything taste better on skewers?*

String assorted raw vegetable in bamboo skewers. Serve with puddle of bottled salad dressing for dipping.

Cucumber, cherry tomatoes, zucchini, carrot rounds, broccoli, cauliflower, snow pea pods, celery chinks, pineapple cubes, bell peppers, all work great

## Asparagus Rafts

Trim 4-6 asparagus spears. Lay flat on table, side by side. Soak bamboo skewers in water at least 30 minutes. Run a skewer through the asparagus, about halfway on the stalks. Do the same with two more skewers, near the top and bottom, building a raft-shape. Brush with Italian dressing. Grill about 4-6 minutes per side.

## Grilled Vegetables

*Delicious served cold, warm, or at room temperature*

Slice zucchini, or other summer squashes, lengthwise. Cut sweet onion into slices. Cut bell peppers into rings or quarters. Toss with bottled Italian salad dressing to coat. Grill vegetables until tender. Drizzle leftover dressing over them. Next time, add mushrooms, green onions, and whatever else you have at hand

## Fruit Skewers and Dip

*Suggestions: banana, apples, kiwi, grapes, melons, berries, pears, mango, stone fruits*

Cut various fruits into cubes, about the size of a grape. Thread on bamboo skewers.

Mix 1 cup sour cream and 2 tablespoons brown sugar. Serve skewers with the dip.

## Warm and Comforting Breads

*These are delicious with breakfast or dinner. Leftovers make fine snacks*

## Orange Peel Muffins

*Eat the orange pulp while the muffin is baking. The cheapest muffin mixes tend to work better ---they're not as tender—and any flavor is fine. The orange peel prevents burning, while adding a nice orange flavor to the muffin.*

Cut oranges in half. Carefully remove pulp, leaving peel intact. Mix boxed muffin mix according to directions on the box, using a zip type bag. Fill peels 3 /4 full of batter. Place in coals, rotating a couple of times, until muffin tests done (poke a clean slim stick into center; it's done when stick is not coated in gooey batter).

## Orange Peel Brownies

*Technically a dessert, but the lines get blurred in the woods.*

Same as Orange Muffins, except use a brownie mix instead. Some mixes require water only—even easier

## Pan Fried Biscuits

*You don't need an oven for this Southern breakfast favorite.*

Stir together 3 cups self-rising flour with enough heavy cream to make a soft dough. Melt 4 T butter in a frying pan, over medium-low heat, tilting to coat pan. Pat dough into the pan, about 3 /4 inch thick. Cook about 5 minutes on each side, turning once, until golden on both sides.

## Oh, My Olive Bread

*Yes, this isn't really cooking; it's cheating. It's also delicious. As long as you are at the local grocery store, you may as well pick up some French bread.*

Slice a loaf of French bread in half, long-ways. Chop up a jar of pimento-stuffed olives, drained, and mix with a heaping handful of grated Parmesan cheese and 4 T butter. Spread evenly on cut side of bread. Put halves together, and wrap loaf in foil. Warm over fire, grill, or near coals, until dinner is ready. Break off chunks. Oh, my

## Sweet Tooth Attack

### (Desserts)

*Even after a satisfying meal, dessert is always a hit Some of these recipes are old favorites, some new treats, all delicious.*

## Almost Instant Rice Pudding

*Creamy comfort food dessert in minutes*

At home, make the mix in a zip-type bag: 1 cup of instant rice, 1/2 cup instant nonfat dry milk, 2 tablespoons sugar, 1/4 teaspoon cinnamon, and 1/4 cup raisins. At camp, add 1-1/2 cups water to the mix and bring it to a rolling boil in a pot, stirring constantly. Remove it from the fire, cover and let it stand, stirring occasionally, 5 minutes.

## Fruit Pie

*A wide variety of foods can be cooked in foil pouches, including desserts. A very easy dessert is fruit pie. This calls for canned pie filling. You can substitute fresh fruit, mixed with a little sugar and dusted with flour, for the canned stuff.*

For each serving, spoon some canned blueberry or apple pie filling onto foil. Add a refrigerated biscuit, and top with more pie filling. Seal foil, leaving an airspace for the dough to expand. Grill until dough is cooked through, about 5-9 minutes, turning a few times.

## Bread Pudding

*Use any kind of berries.*

In a bowl, whisk together 2 eggs, 1 cup milk, 1/2 cup sugar, and 1/4 t cinnamon. Stir in 4 cups bread cubes and 1 cup blueberries or blackberries. Spread on a sheet of buttered foil. Fold in drugstore wrap. Grill over indirect heat, 30 minutes, turning several times.

## Cinnamon Snakes on a Stick

You'll need: Pre-made biscuit dough, or refrigerator biscuits, clean cooking sticks (about 1/2 inch diameter or a bit bigger), and cinnamon-sugar.

Start at the tip of the stick and wrap the dough spiral-style around it, pressing the dough flat against the stick evenly so there are no thick spots. Hold the stick over coals, rotating it slowly over the fire until it's a nice, golden brown. Carefully slide off stick. Top with butter and cinnamon sugar.

## Campfire Peaches

Cut a ripe peach in half, and remove pit. Fill hole on one side with brown sugar-cinnamon mixture, and 1 /2 tsp butter. Reassemble peach, then wrap in foil. Roast in hot coals until slightly softened, about 15 minutes, turning a few times. Careful—they're very hot

## Campfire Mini Pineapple Upside-down Cake

Slice a cake donut in half. As if making a sandwich, add 1 slice canned pineapple, and sprinkle with 1 T brown sugar. Place a maraschino cherry in the center. Wrap in foil and place in the coals or on a grill. Heat through, turning a few times.

## Dirt in a Bag

*Gummy worms, bugs, centipedes, even lobsters are all properly disgusting for this dessert*

Mix any flavor instant pudding according to package instructions in a zip-type plastic type bag. Seal out as much air as possible, and agitate/squish/toss bag until pudding is totally mixed. Add in a few spoons of crushed chocolate cookies, and some gummy critters.

## Snow Camping Ice Cream

*Use fresh snow Yesterday's crunchy stuff isn't nearly as good*

Combine 1 can evaporated milk, 2 T sugar, and 2 t vanilla extract in a bowl, stirring to dissolve sugar. Drizzle a few spoons of milk mixture over individual bowls of packed fresh snow. Eat right away

## Donuts

*Test the oil's temperature: if a bread cube cooks brown pretty fast without burning, it's in the right range. A clean stick or skewer is ideal for turning; slip it through the hole*

refrigerator biscuits
cooking oil
dry flavored gelatin

OR
sugar (cinnamon-sugar, white, or powdered)

Poke a hole through each biscuit with finger, stretching to hold hole open. Drop carefully into 350 degree oil. Flip over when brown, about 40 seconds. Remove from oil, drain on paper, dip into sugar, or gelatin. Best served warm.

## Campfire Éclairs

*Pass the paper towels—you're going to need them*

Pat a refrigerated biscuit into a slug-shape, about a finger in diameter and 4-5" long. Coil around the end of a clean peeled green stick. Toast over coals of a campfire until golden. Twist slightly to remove from stick.

Fill hole with instant vanilla pudding (premixed in a zip-type plastic bag according to instructions on the box). Cut hole in bag's corner to squirt pudding into éclair. Smear canned chocolate frosting on the outside, or dip in chocolate syrup.

## Pudding Cones

*Eat immediately, so the cone won't get soggy. Waffle or sugar cones are sturdier than cake cones.*

Mix any flavor instant pudding according to package directions in a zip-type plastic bag, squishing to combine. Spoon into ice cream cones, and sprinkle with chocolate chips.

**Variation:** stir cut- up fresh fruit into pudding before assembling cones. Use almost any fruit; watermelon is too wet, but berries and stone fruit are delicious

## Cinnamon Snowflake Crisps

*Remember the paper snowflakes you made in first grade? Same concept here.*

Barely warm a flour tortilla over the grill to soften. Carefully fold a tortilla in half, then in half again, without sharp creases. Cut like snowflakes, leaving a part of each fold intact. Spray with cooking spray or lightly butter. Sprinkle with cinnamon and sugar. Toast on grill or griddle until just starting to brown. Mmm....

## Oh, No, It Melted Dessert Bars

This came about on a very hot camping trip, when the s'mores ingredients melted; the marshmallows into a solid blob, the candy bars into liquid. Saving the day, a resourceful adult quickly threw it in a pot, and finished melting it together. Meanwhile, a child was assigned to smash the graham crackers into bits, not crumbs, about dime-size. When the chocolate-marshmallow mixture was smooth, the graham crackers were stirred in, and the whole mess dumped into a shallow pan, and patted flat, a' la rice krispie treats bars. *Delicious*

## S'mores...

Toast a marshmallow in a stick over coals until golden. Sandwich between two graham crackers with half of a standard thin chocolate bar.

## ...and Variations

Besides the usual graham-chocolate- bar –marshmallow combination, try using chocolate covered graham crackers, fudge-striped cookies, chocolate chip cookies, snickerdoodles, or thin granola bars instead of the regular graham crackers. Caramel-filled candy bars are tasty. You can include peanut butter, strawberry slices, and pineapple slices as well.

## S'macos

*the discussion goes on; are these really better than S'mores?? They're really really good!*

Sprinkle one flour tortilla with about 2 T chocolate chips and several mini marshmallows. (not too many –these are very messy!) . Heat on griddle or grill until chips are glossy. Fold to eat.

## Plastic Bag Spoon Fudge

*Eat it with a spoon*

- 3 oz cream cheese
- 1 lb  powdered sugar
- 3 packets of hot cocoa mix or 1/2 cup baking  cocoa
- 2 tablespoons butter

Place all ingredients in a large zip-type bag, and seal with all of the air squeezed out.  Squish and squeeze the contents until thoroughly combined.

## Rice Krispie Treats  (single serving)

Melt 1/2 tablespoons butter in a pot.  Add in five marshmallows, stirring over heat to melt. Remove from heat. Stir in 1 cup Rice Krispies.

## Tiny Cookie Pizzas

*these are really pretty—and tasty They are also time consuming, a fine task for campers while dinner cooks.*

sugar cookies or vanilla wafers

cream cheese thinned with a little honey and vanilla extract

fruits cut into tiny interesting shapes; thin slices, ovals, bits, etc

Spread cream cheese mixture on wafers, then artistically top with fruit.

## Cold Fried Eggs

*If you arrange these carefully, this quick dessert looks like fried eggs on toast*

Arrange a canned peach half, cut side down, on top of a heaping spoon of whipped cream on a slice of pound cake.

## Very Nearly Thin Mints

*Fashion a double boiler by placing a bowl over a pot of simmering water. Easy You could also make a pile of these at home.*

1 box Ritz-type crackers
1 bag dark chocolate candy melts, or dark chocolate chips
peppermint oil

Melt the candy in double boiler. Add several drops of peppermint oil to the melted chocolate. Dip crackers, one at a time, in chocolate/mint mixture. Place on waxed paper to set.

## Fancy Pineapple Cake In Foil (serves 4)

Spray 4 foil squares with cooking spray. Slice store-bought pound cake into 8 slices. Place one slice of cake on each foil. Divide can crushed pineapple over cake. Top each with a spoon of brown sugar and a thin slice of butter. Set another slice of cake on each. Wrap foil in drugstore fold, and heat on grill or on embers until heated through, turning a few times. Open carefully; they drip

## Fruit Pie

For each serving, spoon some canned blueberry or apple pie filling onto foil. Add a refrigerated biscuit, and top with more pie filling. Fold in drugstore fold to enclose, leaving some airspace for expansion. Cook over medium heat until dough is cooked through, about 5-9 minutes, turning a few times.

## Grilled Banana Boats

*Oh, yum*

Slice open a banana lengthwise, through the peel. Pull apart gently and sprinkle mini marshmallows, and chocolate chips between the banana sides. Wrap it in foil, peel and all, and put on the fire coals for a short time to let everything melt. These are also great with peanut butter chips, coconut, drained bottled cherries, or whatever toppings you can think of

## Angels on Horseback

*An old favorite, that tastes better than it sounds Who named this, anyway?*

Dip day-old bread cubes in sweetened condensed milk. Roll in shredded coconut and roast on a stick over coals until golden.

## Campfire Dessert Cones

*Hand-held gooey goodness, easily made for a crowd, assembly-line style*

Spread peanut butter inside sugar-type ice cream cones. Mix chopped bananas, mini marshmallows, and chocolate chips, and fill each cone with mixture. Wrap each cone in foil, and warm over coals or grate, turning every so often. Careful—filling is hot

## Campfire Baked Apples (version one)

Core one apple per person. Fill hole with cinnamon red-hot candies, wrap in foil, and cook over medium coals until tender, pinching with potholder to test doneness

## Campfire Baked Apples (version two)

Core apple, leaving bottom intact. Fill hole with 2 T brown sugar, a slice of butter, 1/4 tsp cinnamon, and some raisins. Wrap in foil. Bake on coals about 15 minutes, until it feels soft when pinched with a potholder.

**a Plea:**

Good for you, taking time to make memories with children, either your own, or those in a group  Camping is awesome, and a healthy break for our electronically addicted nation. I hope you find some new favorites in my book. More importantly, I hope it inspires you to take time with the kids in your life, to teach and enjoy them

**Please take time to leave a five-star review of this book. It'll take you under four minutes, and can be anonymous if you'd prefer.  I greatly appreciate it**

Thanks!

Other Books by Deb Graham

**The Cookie Cutter Legacy**

**Murder on Deck**   a cruise novel

**Peril In Paradise**   a cruise novel

**Tips From The Cruise Addict's Wife**

**More Tips From The Cruise Addict's Wife**

**Mediterranean Cruise With The Cruise Addict's Wife**

**Alaskan Cruise by the Cruise Addict's Wife**

**Hand  Me That Hand Pie!**

**How To Write Your Story**

**How To Complain...and get what you deserve**

**Hungry Kids Campfire Cookbook**

**Kid Food On  A Stick**

**Quick and Clever Kids' Crafts**

**Awesome Science Experiments for Kids**

**Savory Mug Cooking**

**Uncommon Household Tips**